Effective
Employee
Communications

Other books by Michael Bland

Be Your Own PR Man (Kogan Page)
Promoting Yourself on Television and Radio (Kogan Page)
PR Opportunities in the National Press (Michael Bland
Communications)
A Pig at the Wheel (Arrow)
A Bigger Pig at the Wheel (Arrow)

Other books by Peter Jackson

Corporate Communication for Managers (Pitman)
The House Journal Handbook (The Industrial Society)

Effective Employee Communications

Michael Bland
and
Peter Jackson

KOGAN
PAGE

First published in 1990 by
Kogan Page Ltd,
120 Pentonville Rd, London N1 9JN

Printed and bound in Great Britain by
Typeset by J&L Composition Ltd, Filey, North Yorkshire

British Library Cataloguing in Publication Data

A CIP catalogue record for this book is available from the British Library.

ISBN 0–7494–0140–0

Contents

Acknowledgements

Our sincere thanks to the many colleagues and organisations who have helped with their expertise and contributions. They include: Phil Ashcroft (*Sun*); Yvonne Bennion (Industrial Society); Tat Boddye (Ford Motor Company Ltd); Confederation of British Industry; Robert Head (*Daily* and *Sunday Mirror*); International Association of Business Communicators; Institute of Public Relations; John Mayhew (Infovision Ltd); Derek Stone (Ford Motor Company Ltd).

Notes

- 'What does it cost?' is often the first question when considering a new communication method. This book tries to answer that question at each stage but prices can vary enormously according to who and what you use. However, we thought it would help to give at least a 'ball-park' figure based on experience.
- All references to 'he', 'his' or 'him' relate to both sexes and are written solely for convenience and concise English.

Introduction

We've been trying to communicate for hundreds of thousands of years. But we're still not very good at it – especially in business and industry, where there's often less communication among the team doing the job than there was between a pack of our grunting ancestors round a trapped Mastodon. In recent years, however, communication has become more of a buzzword, and many companies devote a great deal of time and money to improving their employee communications. There's also an abundance of courses and publications on the subject. So why *this* book? The answer is that it fills an important gap.

There are many books and other sources of advice on the *theory* of communication, and on all the legal and social aspects. Similarly, there are many sources of help on individual aspects of the *mechanics* of communicating – audio-visual techniques, employee reports, and so on.

This book doesn't try to compete with either group. If you want in-depth analyses of communication theory, trade union aspirations, industrial democracy, or legislation on disclosure, there are plenty of places to find them. But usually these sources leave you hanging just as you're getting interested.

Many will expound on the virtues of having a house journal, for example, but they don't tell you *how* to write it, *who* writes it, how to find a good *printer*, where to get help with the *layout*, how to *distribute* it, and what it's going to *cost*. For that sort of information – covering the whole range of company communication – you'd have to buy a year's supply of reading material going into more depth than you'll ever have time for.

So essentially this book is about *how* to communicate. The second section – which takes up roughly three-quarters of the book – looks at the mechanisms we use to communicate messages and information in companies of all sizes. For each method there's a description of how it works, a look at the pros and cons of that particular method, some pointers to getting started, a rough idea of costs and, very importantly, details of where to go for further advice. Thus it should suit the manager who wants to do more about communicating and is now asking: 'OK, so where do I go from here?' For sadly, considering that it has been some 200 years since the Industrial Revolution, properly structured employee communications is a relatively new art.

The seventies was the decade in which the need for this sort of communication was recognised. It was a period in which Government, with all the fervour of Canute legislating against the tide, enacted law after law to 'try and make industry work'. The decade witnessed the Bullock Report with the consequent emphasis on 'participation' and 'communication' as alternatives to the plan for shop floor directors, and it saw the age of consultation begin in earnest.

The few organisations and companies who, for years, had been preaching and practising good communication became centres of attention, as other less communicative outfits turned to them for an example. It was also the period in which a new wave of communication techniques, notably audio-visual, hit the UK from America. What the new communicators failed to realise, though, was that attitudes are formed by *experience*, as well as *communication*. It's a fat lot of use the chairman's report saying that 'our employees are our greatest asset' if the employee who reads it is given no help the first time he goes to the personnel officer with a problem.

Through the eighties, however, there was a notable improvement in the management of people in some companies, especially when industry had to handle the shedding of large numbers of jobs.

Now it's time to benefit from the lessons of the seventies and eighties and really learn to communicate. One lesson is that the wrong emphasis has often been placed on communication. Unable to face up to the fact that industrial health requires a long struggle and hard work, all parties to the business scene – management, politicians, unions, the press and public – tended to seize on instant cures. It's not that simple. While communication is invaluable it's no substitute for good management, competitive practices, sound industrial relations and plenty of hard work. The key message is that communication must be put into perspective. It is an important management tool, not a panacea for all industrial ills. It rarely achieves immediate results, and it demands a lot of effort.

The second lesson to be learnt from early communicative dabblings by many companies is not to put the cart before the horse. The obvious order of events is: (a) to want to communicate; (b) to have something to communicate; and (c) to find ways to communicate it. All too often, companies start with the latter. They buy elaborate audio-visual systems and publish newspapers with the same lack of sequence as someone buying a record before a record player.

Thirdly, it must be kept up. To start a communications programme and then drop it because it 'isn't working' (ie it hasn't been given time to work, or it's not being done properly in the first place) can do more damage than not communicating at all.

The final important lesson for the future is that communication is really very simple. In an era of microprocessors, video discs, data retrieval and a growing range of complex systems, communication in the last analysis is really only a matter of telling people things.

In *Le Bourgeois Gentilhomme* Molière created the pompous Monsieur Jourdain who hired a professor to teach him to speak prose, when of of course he'd been speaking prose all his life without knowing it. The world of business communication is full of Monsieur Jourdains. In the age of hi-tech communication we must always remember that no amount of sophisticated gadgetry is as good as a word in someone's ear.

Chapter 1
Why Communicate?

The Importance of communication

'Everything would be all right if only we could communicate –
the trouble is we seldom do.'

How many times have managements, facing a possible strike, a
drop in sales or high employee turnover, echoed those words of Jan
Masaryk, sometime Foreign Minister of Czechoslovakia? How
many times have *you* said it, facing bad feeling in your shift or
department, a lack of understanding by higher management of your
own problems, a breakdown in family relationships with your son
or daughter, husband, wife or parents. 'Everything would be all
right ... if only I could make contact, if only I could get them to
understand my position, if only I could explain – *if only I could
communicate.*' The trouble is ... we seldom do.

Communication has been an industrial buzzword for several
decades. In the 1990s you may find it easier to stick to the singular
noun rather than the plural communications which now has an
affinity with telecommunications. Advertise for a communications
manager and you may end up with a queue of computer pro-
grammers at your door, rather than the media relations expert
you seek. Communication has become a professional tree with
many branches: advertisers; public relations experts; broadcasters;
designers; printers, ... but at root it is an essential topic for every
manager. We all have an interest, we are all part of the network.

How much of your time do you spend communicating at work
during an average day? Twenty per cent? Thirty? Forty? Ninety?
We'd all probably agree on a fairly high figure, but even so, as
Masaryk said, perhaps we could communicate more. The important thing is that the communication we *do* make, whatever the
percentage, is effective; that the message gets across, and that
something *happens* as a result. 'I didn't know – nobody tells
me anything.' 'Oh, our communication system failed again.' – as
if communication was something like the national debt or the
electricity grid; something too high and far off for us to influence.
But communication is essentially a *personal* matter – which is why

an increasing number of companies are including it as a subject in their management appraisal programmes. Whatever our present position – supervisor, manager, executive, or director – we *can* improve ourselves and encourage others.

Is your strategy really necessary?

Is all this concern with communicating to employees really necessary? Isn't it just more consultants' jargon? Wouldn't we be better occupied in spending the necessary money and time on improving employee morale (which hasn't really recovered from those redundancies last autumn), or on pushing our products harder in national and trade press advertising (have you *seen* what our rivals have done?), or improving the number of language graduates in the next intake (we'd better get prepared for the Single Market)?

The answer to all three questions is 'yes'. But how exactly are you going to raise morale without telling employees about current plans and future prospects? How are you going to get the full benefit from an increased advertising campaign without setting about an internal marketing programme? And how, with multi-lingual management graduates being courted by companies bigger and better and wealthier than yours, are you going to express the facts that will persuade them to accept your offer? The answer is with nothing less than strong, imaginative employee communication. And in the 1990s there is a perceptible move in many UK companies to show once again how important it is to put into place a structured employee communications programme.

Indeed, the growing use of the phrase 'internal marketing' suggests that at last employees are being seen actually adding value to the company's profit margin. There is a growing belief that not only is it *right* for employees to have greater knowledge about company finances, but that actual participation in the company's manufacturing and commercial activities will see a return on investment. Look around at the flurry of investment in 'quality' and 'customer care' programmes.

This renewed enthusiasm about communication to employees is also, in part, fuelled by self-interest. The unemployment rate is slowly decreasing, and the shortage of school-leavers and engineering-based graduates for the foreseeable future is now widely accepted. Even now it is said that Norwich Union would theoretically be able to employ every school-leaver from the schools of Norwich. The widening European Market will not only increase competition for UK companies and highlight profit margins, but also make industrial dispute avoidance a top priority. These changes both outside and within industry mean that greater attention has to be directed at the whole state of employee morale and motivation, so a strong communication strategy is essential if both are to be positively changed.

Perceiving the need

There can be no doubt that planned internal communication is an essential part of any manufacturing or service company, since among other things, poor employee communication will lead to:

- a lack of understanding of company objectives;
- the inability to carry out individual jobs to the highest possible standard;
- a lack of perception of consumer demands and competitors' challenges;
- poor relationships with immediate superiors;
- criticism and misunderstanding between different departments and divisions;
- the inability to give frank information to subordinates;
- insufficient appreciation of the need for quality and excellence;
- a preference for quick recource to industrial action rather than more lengthy discussion leading to harmonious solutions; and
- a general lowering of morale.

In diagnosing the cause of communication starvation and applying the remedies we must also remember that not every area of the company structure needs the same medicine. It has always been too easy to lump employees together en masse and serve them a standard recipe of information on a recognisable standard company plate. Attitude research has proved irrefutably what common sense should have seen at the start; that different groups of employees need different information presented in different formats. The most obvious distinction is between management and the operatives and staff whose needs share common headings but vary greatly in the depth and length of information required.

For example, the operatives and staff within a group head-quarters, factory, offices and sales branches might need:

- job-related information in great detail;
- pay and benefits information in great detail;
- as much information as possible on the financial and production targets and achievements of their own unit;
- personal information on those directly above and below them in the line;
- general short-term information on company results and objectives; and
- limited information on group structure and results.

On the other hand, most of the managers will need:

- detailed information on financial and production targets and achievements of their own department and division;
- detailed long-term information on company results and objectives;
- adequate general information on other divisions and on group activities;
- personal information on their peers as well as those they report to and those for whom they are responsible.

This is, of course, by no means an exhaustive list of information needs; the range and scope of information which employees need to know will vary within these broad categories depending on location, responsibility and product group, and whether the individual is a supervisor, junior manager, middle manager, senior manager, and so on. Nor must specialist groups be forgotten. The needs of those in research and development will differ from those in sales, as will those in design from those in manufacturing. Such niche communication techniques will not always be possible, bearing in mind the restrictions on practitioners and the budget within which so many communication departments have to work. Nevertheless, the idea that one single communication programme is sufficient for everyone must be firmly resisted and, if emphasis is to be placed anywhere, it should be on the supervisory and middle management levels, where research shows that there are consistent communication bottlenecks.

Try a little research

Did you notice those ubiquitous words in the previous paragraph – 'research shows'? It is impossible to talk for long about the reasons for communication without entering the door marked market research (MR). Indeed, it will be suggested later in this book that unless we take significant doses of MR before, during and after any communications exercise, the project will at best be incomplete and at worst entirely wasted. But at this early stage when we are still asking the question 'why communication?', published facts and figures provide a good starting block which may be preferable to the heady language of converted consultants or the gut feelings of unbelieving managers.

When we take a look at the current needs, fears and hopes of employees today we find significant areas which need to be addressed through better communication.

- *Job content and satisfaction.* The majority of UK employees seem to be satisfied with their jobs, but morale declines with length of service and commitment to employers tends to be low. Is there scope for improvement by better communication? Certainly.

- *Career patterns.* Employees are unsure about their career opportunities – less than one-third are satisfied. Would an information/appraisal programme help? Definitely.
- *Pay and benefits.* Only 30 per cent of employees are dissatisfied with their pay and 58 per cent are satisfied with their benefits. However, over one-third of people feel they could be earning more if they went to work for a competitor. Is there scope for improving company loyalty through a franker information programme? Without doubt.
- *Communication.* It seems that companies are making an effort to talk to their employees, but those employees don't necessarily believe what they are told – 40 per cent say information from management is often misleading. Is there room for improvement? Draw your own conclusions.[1]

We need to communicate because areas like these should be of concern to us as managers – and because the expectations of employees have been significantly raised in recent years both as to the manner of the communication and to what they should be told. If we turn again to the published statistics[2] we find that the topics heading the average employee's information list are:

- the company's future plans;

closely followed by

- job advancement opportunities;
- job-related information;
- productivity improvement;
- personnel policies and practices;
- the company's competitive position; and
- how my job fits into the company.

This is all a far cry from those stories about the sales team's prize trip to Tahiti or birdwatching in Godalming by Denise from bought ledger, which for many years were the sops thought fit to be thrown to information-starved employees! A strong, effective, well-researched and adequately-resourced communication strategy is essential in industry and business today. The rest of this book looks at the scope of the task itself and how to tackle it. But first, a word of warning: For any employee communication strategy to succeed, there must be a firm commitment from board level to the purpose and demands of that strategy, and that commitment must be clearly stated and promulgated. This point has to be heavily emphasised because there is nothing more dispiriting for a company's employees than to have their expectations raised by words from on high, only to find, a year later, that their present state is worse than their first.

Of course many leading management figures have come out strongly in print to make the case for better internal communication.

Goldsmith and Clutterbuck's *The Winning Streak* (Penguin, London) shows many examples of the leadership of UK chief executives in this field as does Peters and Watermans' *In Search of Excellence* (1982, Harper and Row, New York) for their US counterparts. 'When employees learn more from their union representatives than from their management' said Sir Kenneth Corfield, then speaking of the communication regime at STC, 'the power structure is distorted. To communicate is to commit and to commit is to assume responsibility.'

Such printed proclamations of top support of internal communication must be proven both on the shopfloor and in the office.

Not every Chief Executive Officer who is given star billing in the management press actually puts the published statement of intent into practice like Sir Kenneth Corfield. But such pronouncements, for whatever reason they are uttered, *do* help the internal communicator in the uphill task of convincing managers across the company, particularly in the middle, that communication is central to the company's activities and *not* an optional extra.

The bottom line

Back in the days of punch cards, John Garnett of the Industrial Society told of an interview he had with an operator who sat there, day after day, doing a mundane repetitive job for a giant company. She was bored out of her mind and utterly demotivated. Her morale was non-existent and therefore she had a highly detrimental effect on the morale of anyone inside and outside the company with whom she came into contact. During the interview it transpired that the extent of her knowledge of the company was its name and a vague idea of some of its products. When Garnett started to explain the vital role of her particular job in the success of that company's products, and the value of those products to society and the economy, her face started to light up. No one had ever told her before!

More recently, in an organisation whose morale and productivity could most kindly be described as abysmal, a survey of middle managers showed that a substantial percentage did not regard it as part of their job to communicate with their staff. Indeed, many did not even know who all their staff were!

So, the simple bottom line is as follows. When employees are told what is going on, and management shows that it cares, they feel more involved. When they feel more involved they work better, cause less trouble and stay longer. And when employees work better, cause less trouble and stay longer the company makes more money and the organisation is more successful. Sadly, common sense and good old-fashioned altruism are still not enough for many outfits. But more money and success must surely be a sufficient incentive for *every* company and organisation to take employee communication seriously.

References

1 Information taken from the *Work UK* nationwide survey by the Wyatt Company 1988.
2 Companies survey undertaken by TPF&C and the International Association of Business Communicators 1988.

Chapter 2
Who and Where

Different sized companies – management and shop floor

Talking to people is something which should permeate right through any company, of any size, in any line of business and, at all levels. Nor does it apply only to business and industry. It's as important for people to communicate over the breakfast table, at a PTA meeting or on the football field as it is in the factory or office.

Since there's no magic in it, and because it's really only a matter of remembering to tell people what's happening, there's no reason why we shouldn't communicate at all levels as naturally as we drink tea or draw our wages. There are no boundary lines. The size of the organisation makes a difference to the type of communication. With up to about 15 people communications can be informal. Thereafter they need to be more planned and structured. There is another break-point at around 90–100 employees, where morale problems soon develop in the absence of an employee communications programme. Let's look at how it can work in companies of different sizes.

The Hogback saga

When his father died Herbert Hogback left his job to try with the help of his wife Marigold to make a success of the family's ailing corner newsagents. Now Herbert and Marigold run the show between them and pay half a dozen schoolboys to deliver the papers each morning.

In running the shop they communicate all the time without even realising it. It doesn't take a degree in management science to come out with statements like:

- 'They haven't sent enough copies of the *Mirror* this morning, dear.'
- 'If we're going to afford a new sweet stand we'll have to get Acacia Avenue to pay their bills quicker.'
- 'Tom, when you've finished your round don't forget to drop in on Billy and remind him not to come in on Monday because it's a Bank Holiday.'

All very simple stuff. Painfully obvious, in fact. Yet it's this run-of-the-mill, everyday exchange of information that we're talking about. Herbert and Marigold work well as a team – and the newsboys are a happy bunch – because they know what's going on. Each person contributes his or her share of the work more efficiently and willingly by knowing what's going on in the business as a whole. It's important for Marigold to know that Herbert has VAT problems and is going to pay an accountant to help with the books. And it's equally important for the delivery boys to have a word with the proprietors if they think they deserve a pay rise or if a bicycle chain has gone rusty.

Communication in a very small outfit tends to happen naturally, and is of paramount importance. Even in our little corner newsagents things quickly go wrong if communication is forgotten. Like the day Marigold re-arranged the payment books from address-order to name-order, and forgot to tell Herbert. Or the bright lad who went to work for the newsagents down the road because he thought the other delivery boys were being paid more but didn't like to ask if it was true. And even at this level of business there's a need for a more general sort of social communication – the means by which you get to know and understand the people you work with. What in a big company might be the general tittle-tattle in the company newspaper, is exchanged between Herbert and Marigold while they're unwrapping bundles of newspapers.

Fortunately, Herbert Hogback hasn't forgotten the value of keeping people informed when, after ten years of hard graft, he is successfully running his own medium-sized printing company, H & M Hogback (Printers) Ltd. In addition to Marigold he has three co-directors. A team of 15 managers is responsible for a total of 300 employees in two printing works. The directors lunch every day in the boardroom and chat generally about all aspects of the business. Once a week he holds a meeting with all the managers to brief them on developments in the company, explain what needs doing and answer questions. The managers in turn talk things over regularly with the printers, compositors and other staff under their command. So everybody talks to everybody else and it's a happy little company. All the same, Herbert is conscious of the fact that he can't get time to get round the works as much as he should. Last time he looked in on the print room there were a few faces he didn't recognise. And with the two locations ten miles apart the employees in one location see very little of those in the other. He finds that communication at all levels takes more effort and discipline on his part and on that of his managers. So he makes the personnel manager responsible for an exercise in staff communication, including a couple of notice boards at each works, regular briefing sessions between managers and their teams during working hours, and a monthly four-page newsletter.

It is no longer possible, as it was with the corner shop, for every member of the team to be in direct touch with each other. So things have a habit of going wrong when people forget to tell each other what's happening. Many niggling little problems can be traced to attitudes and misunderstandings. Though the company is quite small, Hogback and his fellow directors realise that it's no longer enough to rely on chats over a cup of tea and communication of the 'Oh, by the way ...' variety. They are learning that communication, like sales, finance or any other part of a business, is something which needs to be administered if it's to be successful.

Fortunately, some years later, Sir Herbert Hogback, chairman of the giant Hogback Enterprises Ltd, hasn't forgotten these lessons now that he commands a nationwide printing and publishing empire. He misses the little chats with Marigold, now Lady Marigold Hogback, who devotes her time to organising charity meetings in the village and pottering round the grounds with a pair of pruning shears. In the years of building up his mammoth company he stuck to the principles learnt in the little corner shop 30 years before. He and his management devote a lot of time to keeping tabs on the subsidiaries up and down the country. But he's more and more conscious of the distance between himself and the faces he sees from time to time on his brief visits. Homely chats with all 19,000 employees are out of the question, and even the individual companies are so big that they have to work hard at communicating. In order to maintain something of the mutual understanding, so prevalent in the little team back at the shop, he's had to devote a lot of time and effort to working out how the corner shop type of communication can work in a big company. Very simply, as is his style, he's charted the main groups involved in communication:

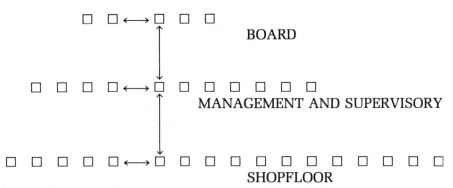

Even with the minimum number of 'layers' (note that he doesn't allow the unions to be an extra layer between management and shopfloor) he finds that communication doesn't flow naturally in any direction and it needs a good shove to keep it going (except of course for gossip and rumour which sweep through all 'blocks' and levels like a dose of flu). He finds, too, that the management layer in the middle filters information on its way down from the board to the shopfloor, and blocks it altogether on the way up from the shopfloor to the board. So he sets up some mechanisms to distribute information among the layers.

The first thing he finds is that it's relatively easy to establish a direct line from the boardroom to the shopfloor. By means of a company newspaper, an employee report and a few of the other methods discussed later in this book, he is able to tell all employees what's happening in the company, what it's earning, what it's producing and where it's going. But it's a very difficult job to get any sort of two-way flow going. He can't tell if his messages are understood or even if they're the right messages. In fact, he's rapidly learning that many companies who pride themselves on their elaborate 'communication' are really only good at sending it one way. It's like a tennis player without an opponent, serving aces and priding himself on his game. When it comes to communication naturally, the managememt layer hit the net so many times that they lose the match by themselves. But with a bit of incentive – and the example set by the few managers who are good communicators – the link between management and shop floor is maintained. By encouraging factory newsletters, effective notice boards and regular briefing groups, for example, the workforces in the individual plants and departments are kept well informed, and once the joint works committees and suggestion schemes get going, there's plenty of feedback.

Sir Herbert is also acutely aware that good communication between the top and middle management is vital but terribly neglected. The 'them and us' attitudes between director and middle manager is as prevalent as it is between management and shopfloor, although it's less noticeable – and less newsworthy. To make it worse, most of the communication methods – such as videos and the company newspaper – which are aimed at the shopfloor, are often too simplified for middle management. So the link between top and middle management needs to be more subtle, although still as much a discipline as the other links. Worst of all are the links between the individual blocks in each level. For Sir Herbert, many a long putt at the fourteenth on a Sunday morning is taken up with the question: 'How do I get them to talk to each other?' This is really difficult. Two employees who stand beside each other on an assembly line talk to each other, but do they talk to their opposite numbers three workstations away? And what incentive is there for the assistant sales manager to swap notes with the data processing manager? That kind of communication is really hard to stimulate. Individuals can't start sending each other

newsletters or presenting informational slide shows to their neigh-
bours at work.

There's no easy answer, and it would be misleading to suggest
methods. But undoubtedly people are more communicative with
each other when they feel involved in what they're doing. And they
start to feel involved when the basic upward and downward
communications are working well. One follows the other. In short,
the question 'who and where' is answered by 'everyone and
everywhere' – at all levels and between all people. But as we've
seen, it's not as simple as it appears. Each level and each link needs
its own special treatment.

One thing that does help is to make some individuals responsible
for communication at different levels through the company. For
example:

- public relations director;
- personnel manager;
- internal communication manager;
- house journal editor;
- personnel/industrial relations managers in subsidiaries/factories;
- personnel officers;
- supervisors;
- 'correspondents' for house journal/newsletters;
- sports/social club secretaries, etc.

With this sort of structure – and it can vary enormously – all
employee levels are covered by individuals whose job it is to
communicate and who, therefore, have to remember to pass information up, down and sideways. It's important to note that this isn't
a formal structure. The people on the list don't necessarily answer
to the ones above them (eg the factory personnel manager will
hardly answer to the house journal editor), but the important point
is to cover the field. Note also that making individuals responsible
for communicating doesn't relieve the others of their obligation to
do likewise. It's the job of *everyone* to remember to communicate
all the time. The appointed communicators are simply there to
promote more system and discipline in the communication process.

There's also the role of two other groups in the communication
process to consider.

Trade unions

Unions do many important things in business and industry, but
they can't be expected to carry responsibility for communicating
between management and shopfloor. It's not their job to be the
purveyors of management messages, nor should they have to report
on the works football results. No self-respecting union should

stand in the way of a genuine company communication programme so long as the union is consulted and kept informed. Nothing should be told to employees that hasn't been told to the union leaders – beforehand if possible – and the communications system mustn't be used for propaganda or for trying to bypass the unions in their proper roles.

They may do battle over many aspects of industry, but so long as tact and common sense are used there's no reason why management, unions and employees can't live together when it comes to the all-important job of communication for the benefit of everyone.

Consultants

Many people are cashing in on the 'communication wave' by setting themselves up as communication consultants. While there is some truth in Robert Townsend's dictum that consultants are people who borrow your watch to tell you the time, an experienced consultant can be invaluable for spotting the areas where you're weakest, establishing a communication programme and using his experience with other companies to point out the things you didn't know or hadn't thought of.

That said, always remember that it's *you* who's doing the communicating, not the consultant. By all means have an adviser leaning over your shoulder, but use him only for advice, ideas and for extra resources when they are needed. Always remember that no amount of consulting relieves you of an ounce of your own responsibility for good communication.

Chapter 3
What and When

It often happens. A company sets up the most elaborate communication system, then it starts to wonder what to communicate. The ideal order of events for effective communication should be:

- wanting to communicate;
- having a message;
- communicating it;

That's not as trite as it sounds. There are plenty of people who don't want to communicate but who have a message to get over, and there are plenty of others who communicate but don't have a message.

As a general rule each communication exercise should consist of one main message and a few subsidiary ones. People can't assimilate great laundry lists of information. The temptation is to say 'Oh yes, I must tell them that ... then while I'm about it they ought to know so and so ...'. If it's a video programme about the annual report and accounts, and you tack on an extra item about the new shift system and a couple of safety messages, there's not much chance of anyone remembering how much you earned last year – which is what you set out to tell them in the first place.

Subjects

Assuming you're happy about the first of those links in the chain – wanting to communicate – it's a useful exercise from time to time to list the things which ought to be communicated in your company. Some will be priority items, such as an impending takeover and what it will mean for jobs, and there may be new products, processes, and premises. At intervals annual figures, pay negotiations and other such information will need to be communicated. There will also be details such as how competitors are doing, long-term plans, or how the company's pension scheme works, that you will want to convey at some time or other. The list will be subject to additions and deletions all the time. For each subject you then need to establish the main message, the subsidiary messages and the general content as follows:

Subject	Competition.
Main Message	Our competitors are getting bigger and better.
Subsidiary Messages	Their quality is improving faster than ours. We are in danger of losing market share. We have the means to beat them. More effort needed by all.
Contents	Review of main competitors – compare their products to ours. Developments in quality and how they measure up to us. Increasing productivity plus quality plus aggressive selling makes inroads into our market share. Our weapons to combat them are product plans, quality control, sales force recruiting. Extra 5 per cent effort by all – manual, sales, management – will get us back on top.

What do they want/need to know?

'Oh, they don't need to know that.'

'What's the point of telling them?'

'If you tell them that, they'll all want one.'

These are some of the favourite cries of the people for whom communication is a dark and secret art. In reality they are simply euphemisms for 'I can't be bothered'. If in doubt about whether employees should be told something or not, why not let *them* judge for themselves? A company takes a big step forward when it starts looking for reasons *for* telling its employees something instead of scratching round for reasons *not* to tell them.

Types of Information

While you should never stick it in pigeon-holes, information comes in two broad categories – 'operational' and 'informational'. The first is the flow of information essential to running the company, while the second covers all the stuff that people either need or want to know.

Operational

Before 'communication' became a vogue word, operational information was what communication was all about. The only communicative skill required of management was to issue operational procedures, manufacturing instructions, shift allocations, safety notices and all the thousands of bits of information needed to run the company. This, of course, is still a vital discipline and it is more immediately crucial to the company's survival than the sort of employee communication this book is about. However important it is for people to be kept in the picture about last year's profits and the inter-company football match, it's even more vital that they know which buttons to press, when to arrive for work and where to go if there's a fire.

But there's plenty of overlap with the second type of information, particularly in the methods used. A notice board, for example, could well carry two notices side by side, one telling employees of the company regulations on safety spectacles and the other announcing an angling competition. One item is operational, the other informational. Or the company newspaper might carry an item about a method for drawing pay by credit transfer. This particular item is probably both operational and informational (as are many) and the company newspaper, while mainly informational, is suitable for both types.

Informational

We're really concerned, however, with the type of communication not directly essential to the running of the company, but which is assuming increasing importance. More and more people want to be kept in the picture. They want to know about the internal and external factors which affect the security and nature of their jobs – like new technology, expansion or layoffs, pay, conditions, food and facilities. They want to know how the company is doing, how much it's making, what new products are in the pipeline, and where it's going. And they want to know about people – other factories, other jobs, new faces, and who's retiring.

Check list

The most useful check list of information to be communicated is the one you compile for your employees. But it's also helpful to back this up with a complete 'laundry list' of things which should or could be communicated. Quite a few organisations have compiled such lists, including ACAS and the TUC. Indeed, several items of information ranging from safety to pension schemes must be disclosed by law. An excellent guide to these is An Employer's Guide to Disclosure of Information by G. Terry Page (Kogan Page). But feeding employees with mandatory information gives them a very scanty diet. There are hundreds of other important things to communicate. Some sources, such as the British Institute of Management (BIM), have done a lot of work assessing which companies convey what information. One very sensible and useful list appears in a CBI Booklet Communicating with People at Work. It breaks the areas of information down into progress, profitability, plans, policies, and people – as follows:

Progress

- Product sales
- market shares
- trading position
- contracts gained/lost
- circulation figures
- cost comparisons
- export sales
- competitors' products
- inflation
- quality index
- safety comparisons
- productivity figures
- development of subsidiaries
- financial results
- safe driving awards
- accident record
- order position
- company achievements
- new products
- prices of raw materials
- fuel and electricity costs
- departmental performance

Profitability

Company income

- Sales and charges to customers
- Income from other sources, eg investments. (It is important to define these sources and not cover them with some vague terms which cloak your information in a kind of mystique.)

Distribution of company income

- Materials – broken down into main headings.
- Wages and salaries.
- Depreciation – illustrated by one or two simple examples.
- Interest – with an explanation on why the company borrowed what it borrowed.
- Other costs – again, it is important to define these.

Net company profit

- Dividends – explain why they have to be paid.
- Transferable to reserves.
- If possible, it also helps if the way in which a unit or profit centre made its particular contribution can be put over.

Added value

Plans and polices

- Health and Safety at Work Act
- supervisor development programme
- power crisis
- expansion plans
- board-level decision affecting work groups
- industrial relations statement
- takeover merger
- payment systems
- job evaluation exercise
- reduction in staff
- sick pay changes
- factory reorganisation/ extension plans

- introduction of consultative committees
- re-organisation of distribution depots
- pension scheme
- advertising policy
- employee car purchase plan
- setting up of property division

- employee savings schemes
- drivers' insurance
- explanation of disputes affecting supplies
- National Insurance contribution change
- common market
- pay bargaining rules

People

- appointments
- resignations
- promotions
- international vacancies
- relocation of personnel
- timekeeping
- absenteeism

- long service awards
- labour turnover
- overtime/short time
- grievance procedure
- training courses
- staff handbook
- job security

And lastly there's one very important message to communicate. It belongs at the end of every checklist. It should be remembered after every production improvement, every suggestion scheme award, every annual report, and every charity collection. It's not communicated enough and can seldom be communicated too much. *Remember to say 'Thank You'.*

When

The short answer to 'When do we communicate?' is 'All the time'. But there are some questions of timing to think about. Whenever possible, let the employees be the first to know. Many an industrial problem has arisen because the employees (management included) have learned something for the first time when they've opened their newspapers.

If you're going to be taken over, or are building a new factory, sacking 10 per cent of the workforce, selling a new product or announcing record figures, it's best for the people who work for you to get the full story from the horse's mouth rather than pick up a mutilated version in the press or on the grapevine. Sometimes it's dangerous to risk a leak of delicate information, in which case every effort must be made to tell the employees at the same time as the official announcement and not a minute later. Generally it's better to take a few risks and entrust them with your confidence. Any possible disadvantages are usually outweighed by the trust and goodwill generated between company and employees as a result of being open and honest.

Some items of information crop up regularly or are known about in advance, so a programme can be drawn up well ahead of time. Obvious examples are the announcement of the annual figures, the launching of a new product, pay rises and top management change. Anyone responsible for communicating in a company should have a diary and/or wall planner, with the dates and timings for the release of information to employees entered in the diary or plan, as soon as they're known about. This has two big advantages: first, it enables you to plan your all-important *lead time*. Most methods of communication need a certain amount of preparation time – some taking longer than others. A video, from inception to editing, can take well over a month. A company newspaper needs between a day and a month, depending on the amount of writing, layout and printing. Even a simple works newsletter takes a couple of days to put together, duplicate and distribute. When sufficient time is given to a communication exercise it stands a chance of being done well. But if it's frantically cobbled together at the last minute it's in trouble from the start.

Secondly, keeping a diary imposes some vital *discipline*. However rewarding and exciting, communicating is a chore and almost all communication exercises become last-minute panics because of a lack of planning! So most communication should be planned and timed like any other managerial exercise, while all *ad hoc* material – such as the pensioners' bingo evening or the fire in the packing bay – should be communicated as soon as possible after the event.

How often?

There's also the question of *how often* you should communicate.

There seem to be two schools of thought on how often employees should be told something. There's the type who tells them once and assumes that a 100 per cent retention will be automatic. And there are those who believe in repeating the message *ad nauseam* in the hope that it'll sink in eventually. These are, of course, the two extremes. The answer lies between them and there are no set rules.

Some things only need to be said once (such as the annual figures), although of course the message may be duplicated in different media. For example the figures could be communicated by means of an employee report, a video, local presentations and the company newspaper. Other things need to be said regularly. People have to be constantly reminded about safety, for instance, and the suggestion scheme could do with a boost from time to time, with a piece in the house journal and a picture of a happy winner holding his cheque. Other items repeat themselves, but may not need a regular boost in the same way as the suggestion scheme.

Product details, for example, naturally tend to be repeated in different ways without conscious effort.

There is no set number of times to repeat any one piece of information, and no set frequency. There is plenty of room for manoeuvre between overexposure and consequent boredom on the one hand, and underexposure where people miss the message on the other.

But always remember that it's just when you're getting tired of a particular message that your audience is starting to hear it.

Chapter 4
The Basic Ingredients

Simple as it sounds, the first ingredient of communication is getting the information. Then it has to be converted into good English, and finally communicated.

Getting the Information

Collecting information isn't easy. Busy managers forget to tell you things. It doesn't occur to the football club manager to tell the company newspaper about the latest victory. A frustrated supervisor might seethe over an injustice for months, but not think of telling his superiors. And, conversely, when people *want* to communicate something they'll suddenly swamp you with too much of it. During pay negotiations some managements suddenly become incredibly communicative, while the PR-conscious social secretary at one factory may hog the pages of the company newspaper to the exclusion of the meeker ones.

This means that an information-gathering *system* is needed. It becomes the job of everyone involved in communication not only to pass information *down* the line, but to remember to pass information *up* it. We'll be looking at some ways of doing this in the chapters which follow. Basically there is a need for at least one 'link' person in each department or section to keep in touch with public relations or whoever is responsible for spreading information around the company. It's no use having sophisticated and expensive communication systems without equally disciplined and effective methods of gathering the information in the first place.

Converting It

Having collected the information from the various sources, it's unlikely to be in a form that everyone else can comprehend. People tend to communicate in a language that only they can understand. Engineers and scientists fill their sentences with jargon. Middle management and bureaucrats delight in inserting lots of extra words which they hope will give them an erudite appearance. Favourite 'filler' words currently include 'scenario', 'viable', 'synergistic', 'matrix', 'parameters', 'situation' and a host of other gobbledegook.

As company communicator you might find yourself faced one day with a 'bare-bones' message consisting of basic facts and figures and desperately in need of fleshing out. The next day you might have to interpret this (genuine) gem from a staff circular.

'The actual return fare to the employee's permanent place of employment (or home if less) at the class appropriate to his grade will be allowed plus day subsistence for the period from the end of the 24–hour cycle for night subsistence to the time of arrival at his permanent place of employment (or home) within the limit of night subsistence for the nights of absence over the weekend'.

Here are some basic techniques for turning information into communication:

Simplicity

The only place where you get prizes for long words is at university. If you keep your words and sentences short everyone can understand what you're saying. This often requires more work than the long-winded stuff. Blaise Pascal once wrote at the end of a letter to a friend: 'Sorry this letter is so long. I did not have time to write a shorter one'. Too often we are guilty of being as out of touch as the judge in the famous court case of the Barnsley miner versus the Coal Board. Not convinced that the miner's injury was his employer's fault, the judge asked the plaintiff's counsel: 'Has your client not heard of *volenti non fit injuria?*' He got the answer he deserved: 'M'Lord, in Barnsley they talk of little else!'

Anyone with an interest in communicating doesn't deserve to sleep at night until he has read the masterpiece on how to use the English Language: *The Complete Plain Words* by Sir Ernest Gowers (HMSO). No bookshelf or briefcase should be without it. Another useful source of guidance is to look at the financial columns of the mass-circulation dailies. The journalists who write these columns are past masters at explaining complex material in simple terms.

We tend so often to use long words when shorter ones will do. Here Robert Head, City Editor of the *Daily Mirror* and *Sunday Mirror*, has compiled a useful list of the 'long' words most commonly used by British management, with their 'short' equivalents:

accumulated	built up
acquired	bought (stole)
additions to	more
adequate	enough
borrowings	debts
category	class, type
commissioned	set up
confidence	faith, trust
considerable	big
constructed	built
contributing	chipping in
cost-effectiveness	efficiency
currently	now
demonstrate	show
discovered	found
disposed of	sold
division	part, side
expanded	built up, grew
expansion	growth
experienced	seen
facilities	works
fifty per cent	half
for the manufacture of	to make
in co-operation with	working with
increase	rise
individuals	people
institutions	banks, insurance companies, pension funds
interim	half yearly
in the current year	this year
is responsible for	runs
liquid resources	cash
main factor	reason
marketing	selling
minority interests	partners
operational	running
operations	business
organisation	company, firm
overcapacity	glut
pharmaceuticals	medicines
pretax	before tax
reduction	cut, fall
representatives	salesmen
satisfactory	good
surplus	profit
taxation	tax
turnover	sales

Everything you prepare for communication to employees should be subjected to some sort of 'Bullshit' test before it goes out. Get a colleague who isn't familiar with the subject to read or listen to the material to ensure that it's comprehensible. At the very least you should check through it yourself, pretending you're one of the intended recipients.

Relevance

After the 'Bullshit' test comes the 'So what?' test. It's very easy to set up an elaborate communication system with the best intentions, only to find yourself 'communicating' anything and everything because the system demands it.

One American communication manager admits of his company's video network: 'It's a monster. Once we'd created it we had to go on feeding it.' And once people start to receive irrelevant material (one programme on the above-mentioned video system was all about the trade calendars issued by the subsidiaries) they'll soon switch off the whole thing and miss the important bits. So before it goes out, does it pass at least one of four simple tests:

- Do they *need* to know it?
- Do they *want* to know it?
- Is it *entertaining*?
- If none of these, *why* am I sending it out?

Illustration

Wherever possible give examples. Show how things work using pictures, slide or film. 'The new press is the biggest we've ever had' is interesting enough, but how much better when accompanied by a photograph of the giant press with a tiny-looking operative standing beside it. Be it a product, pay rise or pension scheme, give practical examples of how it works and how it affects people.

At the same time watch out that you're not getting carried away with visual aids. I was once told by an army instructor that he'd been involved in a project to reduce malaria in a remote part of the Far East. For months they went from one isolated jungle village to the next, using a 3 ft long model of a female Anopheles mosquito to show how malaria was contracted. Each village was issued with ample supplies of insecticide spray and told: 'Whenever you see one of these, spray the area with this.' A year later malaria was still rife and none of the DDT had been used. It turned out that despite extensive searching the natives had been unable to find a mosquito 3 ft long!

Audience

Do you really know your audience? It's very hard to strike the balance between being too complicated and too patronising. Often the same communication will go to a wide range of people from the boardroom to night security. Others are tailored for particular groups, and this is where the danger of talking down to people creeps in. Certainly, all communication needs to be simple and comprehensible, but only someone who regularly meets and communicates with the various audiences can get the feel of how to express things in the most acceptable way.

Frequency = familiarity = acceptance

You must have heard the familiar cry: 'Oh, we tried that and it didn't work.' The managements of industry are full of people who are prepared to give anything a try ... once. In a burst of enthusiasm, and at enormous cost both in time and money, a new team briefing system is set up, or all the employees are taken off the job once a month to watch the company's new communications on television. When the eagerly awaited leap in profit fails to materialise the scheme is dropped like a hot potato. Yet if you think about it information is more acceptable when we receive it from a *familiar* medium – like our daily paper or favourite television channel. The same is true in industry. Don't start on any sort of communication programme unless you intend to carry on with it.

How to be credible

'We've told them a hundred times but they won't *listen!*' This is the familiar cry of the disillusioned, once well-meaning manager who thinks that he has been doing a good job communicating – but all to no avail. What he has failed to understand is that it isn't enough to simply tell people things. It's *how* you tell them that makes all the difference.

The classic example is Shakespeare's 'Friends, Romans, countrymen' speech in which Mark Antony has the unenviable task of trying to persuade the Roman mob that the highly unpopular Caesar was actually OK and that it's really the popular Brutus who's the villain. If he had just stood there and proclaimed Caesar's virtues he would have joined his late chum in no time. But he didn't. Instead, he tells the crowd what they want to hear ('I come to bury Caesar, not to praise him'). They like that, so they shut up and start to listen. Then, once he's got their confidence and their attention, he gradually starts the successful hatchet job on Brutus.

If only some management teams could adopt a little of this

obvious, simple psychology! All right, so the board actually believes that the drop in production really *is* the fault of the workforce (it probably isn't anyway, but that's another story). But what they must realise is that there's no point in telling the employees they must work harder, until some groundwork has been done, so that they accept that they have contributed to the drop in the first place. Otherwise, hitting any 'audience' with an unwelcome message only reinforces their attitude barriers. To break down an attitude barrier you need to be more subtle and use positive messages, praise, encouragement, and questions. You must listen as well as talk.

I well remember losing a battle to stop a vice-president using the company newspaper to blame the workforce for a long strike and berate them for the damage they had done. To make it worse, his PR head wrote the article in the most appallingly patronising terms, relating the company to a football team in the 'all pull together' mode. All that it achieved, apart from driving an even bigger wedge between 'them' and 'us' was a well-deserved letter from an employee suggesting that it might help if the directors got out of the 'directors' box' occasionally and came down on the 'pitch'!

Conversely, the finest example of motivation and communication I experienced was from a senior Army officer who (a) *asked* his *team* (very clearly) to do something, (b) *thanked* them when they did it, and (c) above all, kept telling them how marvellous they were. People were thus motivated by the irresistible pressure to meet his high expectaions.

So, if you want your employee communications to actually *work* do please remember:

- they are your colleagues – as vital to your success as you are to theirs;
- you are communicating *with* them, not *at* them;
- they respond well to praise and good news;
- they respond badly to criticism;
- when things go wrong there's no shortage of managers to rub their noses in it – but when things go right, no one remembers to thank them;
- don't patronise. Yes, things should be kept simple, but always remember that the apparently semi-literate *Sun*-reading machine operator can also calculate – in five seconds – a pools permutation that would take a computer a week.

Communicating the Information

Having collected the information and turned it into a message, the next job is to go ahead and communicate it. *How* it's communicated will depend on many things – size of audience, facilities, cost and so on. And there are plenty of different methods to choose from. The rest of this book concerns those methods.

Chapter 5
Written Communication

Written communication has a number of advantages. It's less prone to ambiguity and misinterpretation than its verbal counterpart. Distribution is usually simple and effective. It's relatively inexpensive. It's there for posterity and can be re-read as often as you wish.

We receive written information on thousands of aspects of the world around us; not only from newspapers and magazines, but through newsletters, advertisements, forms, hoardings, bulletins, bills, bank statements, books, brochures, letters, leaflets and instruction manuals.

In industry the written word is still the main method of disseminating information, both within the company and to the outside world. The external methods, such as press releases and adverts, are outside the scope of this book. We will concentrate on how we talk to employees on paper.

The main media we will consider are:

- official paperwork;
- information bulletins;
- newsletters;
- company newspapers and magazines;
- employee reports;
- letters, posters and leaflets.

Official paperwork

This sort of communication includes:

- standing instructions;
- office regulations;
- operating manuals;
- memoranda;
- organisation charts;

in fact any written material concerning the running of the company.

The reason they're mentioned here is because they tend to be seen as mere formalities and not as information-providers. Let's take a couple of examples. The regulations in one engineering factory state: '*Hair of machine operatives must be kept above shoulder length.*' A rival company's regulations say: '*Long hair can catch in the machinery with fatal results. It must be kept above shoulder length.*'

If that example sounds trite, just spend half an hour going through some of your internal paperwork and ask yourself how much it really tells its recipients.

While written instructions, memos and manuals must still serve their purpose as operational documents, there are a few simple criteria for improving their effectiveness, clarity and credibility.

Is it necessary?

Is this a ridiculous question? Take your fattest file from the drawer and go through it item by item, asking yourself if anything would have been different if each piece of paper in the file had never existed.

One Scottish insurance company was finally persuaded by its London stockbrokers that it was more efficient to place orders for share transactions on the telephone than by letter. So a few weeks later the brokers received a letter from the client: 'We will telephone you on the 18th inst to place an order for ...'.

The communication lesson to be learnt here is that *if it's merely bumf it doesn't communicate anything.*

Have I explained why?

This is like the example of the long hair and the machinery. There's untold scope for background information to be communicated via documents such as standing instructions. There's a world of difference between: '*Afternoon tea break will now be taken between 3.00 and 3.15 pm instead of 3.30 to 3.45*' and '*Because some machinery has been overheating, afternoon tea break will now be taken at the earlier time of 3.00 to 3.15 pm.*'

Is it clear?

The instructions may be clear in your head. Are they clear to the person reading them? As mentioned in Chapter 4, it's always a good idea to get a third party to run an eye over any document before it goes out, just to make sure it's unambiguous and comprehensible.

Could it be shorter?

Bulky documents are a great turn-off. Almost everything we write could be shorter and thus more likely to be read. But don't throw the baby out with the bathwater! Brevity may be the soul of wit but it can also be the cause of misinformation.

Bulletins

Information bulletins come somewhere between official paperwork and newsletters. Their purpose is to disseminate items of immediate information – such as the results of pay negotiations. If they are distributed regularly, or are lengthy, or contain several items of information then they become effectively newsletters. A typical bulletin might contain details of the latest pay and conditions negotiated between unions and management. It's simple, short and factual, and is put out in bulletin form because it's important information which should reach employees as quickly as possible. The information is prepared by management – possibly in conjunction with unions – and printed and distributed by whichever means is fastest and most effective.

Newsletters

The newsletter is one of the most valuable methods of communication. Its great advantages are that it's simple and parochial. It's no coincidence that newsletters flourish so abundantly in parishes, colleges, and in sports and social clubs of all kinds. They are also highly popular among specific trades, such as catering, finance, housebuilding and car dealing. In America newsletters are so prolific that there's a highly successful newsletter written specifically for newsletter writers!

More than almost any other medium, a newsletter tells people what's going on in their circle of interest, be it a company or an angling club. It is usually cheap and simple to produce, and can contain plenty of information which the large-scale media like videos and newspapers have to omit.

Local news is the most interesting news. That's why there are only 12 national dailies but over 1000 *local* newspapers. What the Council is doing about the pedestrian crossing in the High Street is as important to the resident of a small town as the Prime Minister's resignation. And the fact that your department won the factory darts trophy means almost as much as the company winning a Queen's Award to Industry.

Frequency

A newsletter can be anything from weekly to quarterly, but monthly is ideal. With a monthly newsletter aim to come out as near as possible to the same day each month. A typical schedule might be as follows:

Working day
[1–15]	items put into 'forthcoming issues' file
[10]	ring round department managers, sports and social club, convener, etc to ask for their input
[16–18]	collect material and edit
[19]	print and collate
[20]	distribute to employees

Who writes it?

Ideally, everybody should contribute. In a perfect world the editor's job should be one of chasing the various departments for their contributions, and collating and editing them. In real life you end up writing great chunks of it yourself, but it's a small price to pay for such an effective communication tool. Even if the newsletter only consists of two sides of A4 once a month, and one individual has to write half of it, that's still only ten words a day!

Overall responsibility *must* be in the hands of one person. This will usually be the personnel manager or industrial relations manager of the unit (which for newsletter purposes would be a factory, small company or large department). It can equally well be the job of an assistant manager, PR person, or simply a talented enthusiast. The main thing is that *somebody* is responsible. He in turn can co-opt any number of honorary assistants. The idea is for the person in charge to encourage someone in each section – accounts, football team, marketing, etc – to feed in relevant news and topics. It'll mean constant prodding, but it's worth it when employees are made aware of an important forthcoming briefing meeting, or when Joe Hacker reads about the goal he scored against the buying department last week.

Some part of the newsletter, usually the opening paragraphs, should be the property of the top person in the unit – the factory manager or department head. Apart from involving the manager, steer clear of editorial committees and readers' panels which are the kiss of death for any publication.

Format

A newsletter benefits from being 'homespun'. Use typewritten paragraphs with double line spacing or, if available, a word

Here's a typical two-sided A4 newsletter, printed in-house on a tinted paper with the circular masthead pre-printed. The original was typewritten on a word processor.

A newsletter for Cadbury Schweppes employees at G.H.Q.

CHRISTMAS AT LECONFIELD HOUSE

The Washington Hotel is the venue for this year's Christmas Lunch on December 20th. The menu is a traditional Christmas meal and there will be separate tables for 10–15 people with waitress service.

There is no charge for the lunch this year. You will be sent a ticket which you should bring to the lunch. If you have any special dietary restrictions, please contact Anne Fletcher.

After lunch is over look forward to the *Christmas Party*, which will be held in the snack bar from 5.15 that evening. Details overleaf.

And don't miss *Christmas Lunch* in the snack bar on Thursday 22nd December. Our caterers have planned an excellent turkey dinner. Service will be as usual.

BACK TO MARBLE ARCH

If you have passed our building on Connaught Place recently, you might well wonder how things are getting on. The building still looks in a state of total disrepair.

Rest assured, however, the work is proceeding. All that scaffolding and polythene cover up what is currently happening – which is mostly on the inside. Air conditioning, pipe laying, ceiling work, plastering are carrying on as planned.

WHAT THE PAPERS SAY

Schweppes is spending £900,000 between now and the new year through Saatchi and Saatchi on a national TV campaign, using Channel Four for the first time.

The campaign will comprise four different commercials, three for Schweppes tonic water and a new one for Schweppes lemonade.

CANTEEN QUESTIONNAIRE

Site committee representatives thank you for your co-operation in the recent survey about catering arrangements.

The result of the questionnaire is that most people at Leconfield House want a catering service in-house, but are not particular about the type of service. A minority said they would prefer a service similar to what is currently offered, but the rest indicated that even simple cold snacks would suffice. The committee will investigate whatever alternatives are available and will decide on the most appropriate one, taking into consideration our current needs, usage and length of requirement.

NEW PHOTOCOPIER

A Rank Xerox 1045 photocopier has been installed on the second floor in place of the old one. The new machine will copy up to A3 paper size as well as pre-set reductions. It has automatic paper feeding, a collator, an automatic document positioner and instant start. It can also do double-sided copying.

A training session on the new machine will be held on Thursday afternoon, December 15th. Contact Anne Fletcher if you want to attend.

For your queries and contribution to Leconfield Letter contact Robin McCulloch, Asst Group Communications Manager, Ext 2024. Issue No 3 will appear Monday 9th January.

CHRISTMAS CLOSING

GHQ will be closed on the following days over the Christmas period:

Monday 26 December
Tuesday 27 December
Monday 2nd January.

In addition, at managers' discretion, staff may leave early on Friday 23rd December.

STAFF SHOP
CHRISTMAS OFFERS

There is still a very good selection of tins and boxes of assorted biscuits for Christmas in the Staff Shop. All Staff Shop prices have been reduced by a further £1 on each.

Martin Hammond has asked us to explain that after December 2nd Histon would not accept any further orders for delivery before Christmas. As a result, some lines are low and may run out.

NEWS BRIEF

Forecasters watching the London Tea Auction are predicting that the cost of tea will rise considerably next year because of world-wide shortages. The problem seems to be in the primary producing countries, notably India, where consumer demand has increased sharply. This has reduced the amount available for export.

ADMIN

Anne Fletcher would like to remind all secretaries that if they are unable to contact the chauffeurs for whatever reason, they should contact either Anne on ext 2001 or Sue on 2161.

The chauffeurs have been extremely short-staffed recently due to illness. Anne and Sue are helping maintain an adequate service.

TRAVEL TO
HEATHROW AIRPORT

From Chris Daws – A car or taxi may be the quickest way to reach Heathrow but the A3 airport bus service runs a close second. Advertised journey time is 45 to 50 minutes, but in reasonable off-peak conditions 30 min is nearer the mark. This beats the underground and takes you right to the terminal entrace, with no parking problems. A3 airport buses leave from Park Lane by the Hilton throughout the day until 16.24 at 24/29 and 54/59 minutes past each hour. Fare £2.50.

FOR SALE

Flat for sale, 1 Stamford Hill N.16. £28,950. Large 2-bedroomed flat with wardrobes, fully fitted kitchen with hob and oven, tiled bathroom, fitted carpet throughout. Contact Davina Benito, ext 2054.

SOCIAL

You are invited to the *Christmas Party* in the snack bar on Tuesday, December 20th from 5.15pm. Tickets are £1 and include entrance, free food and one free drink. See your Site Representative for your tickets. Wednesday 30th November will be the last of three short talks headed *Mission to Mayfair* at Christchurch, Down Street, just a minute from the office past the back of the Hilton. These talks are aimed at those who are wondering what the Christian life involves and what it offers. Come at 1.05pm and stay for coffee and sandwiches afterwards. *Peter Jackson*, gingerly web-footing his way about Curzon Street after Saturday's sponsored swim, gratefully thanks those who were rash enough to put money on him. He can only apologise for exceeding forecasts by 100% and managing 40 lengths in 25 minutes!

PEOPLE

Stewart Ross left Cadbury Schweppes on 2 December to join DCBF. *Chris Milburn*, currently Management Services Manager, Bourneville Factory, will join GHQ on 9 January as Group Information Development Manager. *Chris Goodban* moves from GHQ to Export . Division at Dollis Hill as Commercial Manager, reporting to Bert Smith. *Graham Bisacre* leaves to join Stewart Wrightson Holdings on 6 January and will be replaced by *Caroline Bryant* from Export Division on 23 January.

processor is ideal for this job, as is a simple desk top publishing system. Two to four sides – usually A4 – stapled where necessary, are adequate. Any more than four sides and items are less likely to be read – and it becomes more of a headache for the person producing it. Keep the individual items short.

A graphic but simple 'masthead' is effective. To give the news-letter extra identity have the paper pre-printed with a two-colour design strip across the top.

Style

Keep it simple. Use short words and sentences and paragraphs. There will be no marks awarded for long words, long-winded phrases or jargon. Also there is nothing to lose by being frank and open, within the obvious confines of safeguarding company secrets. And it does no harm to admit mistakes occasionally.

What goes into it?

First let the boss have a say, ie the person running the unit in which the newsletter circulates. If you introduce messages from head-quarters the newsletter loses its parochial touch, though interesting material *about* the company is obviously important. It only needs a couple of paragraphs – a sort of message 'from the headmaster's study', only less patronising.

The next section could be production or sales achievements, set against targets – with a word of praise if they've been hit, or with reasons if they've not. There should also be details of the introduc-tion of new processes, the installation of equipment, and any changes and reorganisation of the factory or department.

Keeping within the unit, how about an occasional half page on 'get to know your department', describing the work of sections to those employees not directly involved? Don't forget things like safety campaigns, suggestion programmes and quality control drives. And give some space to union events such as forthcoming meetings and charitable activities.

It'll probably be an uphill task at first, but try to solicit contribu-tions from employees, such as individual views on the unit and their jobs, achievements and experiences. This leads on to the all-important *personal* aspect of the newsletter – births, marriages, deaths, retirements, social and sporting achievements, results of competitions and new appointments. People love to read about themselves and those they know.

You can help the readers by including information about local activities outside the plant which are of interest to the community, such as road repairs, train delays or other items affecting the journey to work, discounts offered by local firms, blood donor sessions and the like. Finally, don't forget to include somewhere the name and phone number of the person to contact with material for future newsletters.

Production

Most units have adequate printing facilities. If not, most towns have small copying firms who can do the job inexpensively. An outside agency can also take care of the dull chore of collating and stapling. But, beware of photocopying. It's very expensive.

Distribution

It's important to distribute copies quickly to all employees. In a small operation a personal hand-out will be possible, while in a large group individuals from each section can collect them from a central point. Some companies mail newsletters and house journals direct to employees' homes. The proponents of this system believe it's more personal that way, and is more likely to be read by both the employee and his family. However, some recipients might regard company mailings as an intrusion on their privacy. It's also a very expensive way of disseminating information. Before mailing to people's homes why not survey their views on the subject. Back at the company the newsletters can be left at distribution points for employees to pick up. It may be possible to use the internal mailing system. Don't forget to pin a copy to the notice board to remind people that it's out.

Check list

Whoever's in charge of the newsletter can make life easier each month with a simple check list. The following example would fit nicely on two sides of an A5 card. The 'info from' lines are for the names and numbers of useful contacts and contributors.

Manager's Message
Production figures   Schedules. Reasons for variance.
Info from:
Mike Moore
Tel: 2315

Personnel   Appointments and changes, births,
Info from: marriages, deaths, sickness. Outside
Justin Holman   successes.
Tel: 3213

Plant Info from: Bill Symans Tel: 3185	Any changes and reorganisation. Production changes; alterations to buildings and facilities. Items affecting work; shifts, systems, catering, safety, suggestion scheme, quality control. 'Get to know your plant.'
Sport and Social Info from: Julie Brown Tel: 1181	Club news; darts, football, etc in-plant and inter plant.
Union Info from: Alf Richards Tel: 4445	Meetings, charity fund-raising, etc.
Community Info from: Mike Hayes Tel: 6626	Road repairs, etc, rates, blood donors, special offers to employees.
Forthcoming Info from: Sandra Dean Tel: 2551	VIP visits, union meetings, etc.
Contact	Name and phone number of person or employee to contact with newsletter material.

Company newspaper

The next stage up from a newsletter is to have your own company
newspaper. But it mustn't be allowed to *replace* the newsletter.
The two have different – and complementary – functions.

A newspaper comes into its own when you have large numbers
of employees. If you only have a few hundred it'll be far too
expensive per employee to produce. There's no firm limit but your
staff numbers should be well into thousands before considering a
newspaper. Newsletters are still needed to satisfy the smaller
groups with all the local details for which a newspaper lacks space.
For instance, the folk in the Lothian branch won't be all that
interested in the appointment of Bill Fogerty as deputy director of
finance at head office. It might get a mention in the *newsletter* but
no more. However, the *newspaper*, circulating round head office
and a dozen subsidiaries, will probably find the information worth
a couple of column inches, with a picture of the new man and some
background information. On the other hand, the fact that Line Four

won the factory darts championship for the third year running is important for the *newsletter*, and the covering item will give all the details of team members and their scores. But in the *newspaper* it wouldn't be fair on the other factories if that particular result took up more than a very brief report.

Few people realise how popular company newspapers and magazines are. The exact number of companies publishing their own journal is unknown, but it's believed to be more than 2000 in the UK alone. That's *twice* as many industrial newspapers as *all* the national, regional and local newspapers put together. If you include those families who read the copy that Mum or Dad brings home, this gives a staggering readership of about 23 million people, which puts all other newspapers in the shade.

A company newspaper is of major benefit to employee communication. It provides a regular medium for information on how the company is doing, what the competitors are up to, new developments and processes, employee activities, features of company and general interest, classified ads, sport, humour, and a whole range of material which would otherwise go by default. Against these advantages must be weighed the cost, which will vary enormously depending on size, frequency, staffing and circulation. However, any company with employees numbering thousands should seriously consider launching a publication. Just as people often get more out of their local paper than they do out of the nationals, so they will appreciate their own company publication and have an affinity with it.

Form and style

The varieties are endless. So much depends on how much time, staff and money you have to put into it, how many people it goes to and what sort of jobs they do.

Some companies prefer a *magazine*. This seems to be most popular among such organisations as banks and insurance companies where a high proportion of staff might be disconcerted by a 20-page tabloid. Magazines have two main assets: the reproduction of type and photographs is of much higher quality than in a newspaper, and it can be issued at lengthy intervals. There's nothing unusual about a magazine coming out quarterly, half-yearly or even yearly, but a newspaper needs to be more frequent. The arguments against a magazine are that it's expensive to produce and is a less familiar medium to most employees than a newspaper.

If you're catering for large numbers at frequent intervals then a newspaper format is the likeliest bet. What sort of format should you choose? There's everything from a glorified newsletter to a full-scale newspaper based on the popular dailies. Some firms start out with a four-page tabloid spread and build up slowly, others start with the full works. Many company newspapers fall into a typical house journal format – on a heavier, glossier paper than the nationals. This has the advantage of higher quality reproduction, though it's also more expensive and less familiar to the reader than the cheaper types of newsprint.

What matters is that the newspaper should be easily handled and read, and that the printing costs are kept within bounds. Common sense should dictate whether a paper is too big and glossy or too small and grubby. Certainly, the paper must *look* readable. Outsiders should want to pick it up and read it when they see it lying on the reception table. And each item should be temptingly presented to make the reader want to read on. The real core of a paper is its contents. Above all, your aim should be to *entertain*. This is a big advantage of newspapers over other methods such as newsletters or bulletins. If it's entertaining then people will want to read it, and if they want to read it then they'll take in the information it contains.

There are books (see the list on p. 65) which go into detail on newspaper style; a world full of 'ems' and 'column inches', 'clashing heads', 'rules', 'teasers', 'hoods' and a thousand other devices that keep sub-editors and designers in employment. But you, too, can be an 'instant expert' by simply taking lots of newspapers and magazines and asking yourself 'which bits appeal to me?' More importantly, bounce the same question off some of the people who are going to read your paper. Using plenty of observation and common sense, keep an eye out in your normal daily reading for the devices that seem to work and for the ones that don't. Remember, too, that you've got time on your side. The wizards of Wapping have to cobble together several editions of thick newspapers every day. You've got weeks to compile yours. You can polish off your instant education by a session with a professional – just to pick up some of the golden 'dos and don'ts' and learn a bit of the language. There are plenty of people you can approach individually and there are many training courses, running from one or two days to a solid week. If you like the look of another company's newspaper, or a local or trade paper, why not ring up the editor and ask if you can go round for a chat or speak to someone else on the staff who could help?

Editorial freedom

It will be counter-productive if you churn out a company newspaper which is no more than an official vehicle for management messages. Employees aren't fools. If your newspaper is stuffed with material of the 'yet another successful launch of a company product took place last week' variety you will be spending an awful lot of money on wastepaper.

The company publication *must* have a high degree of editorial freedom. Whoever's in charge must be experienced, and sympathetic to both sides of each story. It's a trying task. The most difficult thing in the world is to report both management and union views on a contentious issue in a company newspaper. Management has to learn that although they're paying for the paper it's in their worst interests to exercise a journalistic *droit de seigneur* on its contents. And unions must be persuaded that, by giving their views to the company newspaper, they aren't necessarily hobnobbing with 'them'. A balance *can* be achieved. Note, too, that 'editorial freedom' doesn't mean the automatic blacking of anything faintly managerial. So long as they're kept in balance with the rest of the news, stories about the chairman's golf win or the IR manager's explanation of the new shift system are useful and relevant contributions to the paper.

You can even carry the occasional piece of management propaganda so long as it clearly states who wrote it – 'Why the Unions are killing our golden goose – production director Les Grundy gives his views on a burning issue'. It is better still if the piece invites readers' views on the subject and the editor gets in touch with the local convener to respond in the next issue.

Staffing

Some maintain that the company newspaper should be produced 'in house', while others advocate its production by an outside firm. The argument for having it produced by someone else is that it's put together by professionals so that the contents are unbiased – and seen by the readers to be so. Those in favour of producing the paper in-house argue that you need full-time company staff to give the paper the right feel, to root out all the important little stories and make it a truly 'company' publication.

Both arguments have valid points. In many cases the professionals can turn out a much smarter product than company amateurs. Contacts in each department feed information to the agency who then turn it into a lifelike newspaper. But this is really only a halfway house. News of all types has to be gathered, mostly by people who know the scene and know what they're looking for. This applies as much to the names of the winners of the first-aid competition and the losers of the angling trophy, as it does to product descriptions and customer orders. As with so many areas of business, it's best to have your own people to do this job.

A newspaper serving a fairly small company can be done on a modest scale with, say, half a dozen people putting in a couple of days each month on a four-page paper. But a big company, communicating effectively with thousands of employees, should really establish the budget for a full-scale newspaper with full-time staff. A monthly 12–16 pager can be run more than adequately by a team of three or four: an editor, reporter, secretary and someone to look after distribution, advertising and general administration. They must act as a close-knit team and be prepared to interchange jobs when necessary. In addition there should be at least one contact in each location to root out local news. The more of these voluntary 'stringers' there are – especially for reporting on social events, sporting results and stories about people – the better. Of course, the full-time staff will often be engaged on other company duties in the public relations or corporate affairs area and the proportion of their time given to the newspaper has often to be carefully justified and strongly defended.

The approach taken by many large companies is to employ professional journalists as full-time staff to run the company newspaper. This has the double advantage of combining professional expertise with an intimate knowledge of the employees whose paper it is. However, a keen member of staff who has a flair for writing and is prepared to train, *can* make a good reporter – and many have. The vital point is that somewhere along the line the finished product must receive the touch of someone who knows how to produce good 'copy'. The stories themselves *must* be punchy and readable, with plenty of life and pace, and with unambiguous, uncluttered constructions. By all means get the management to provide information, but if they're allowed to write the paper themselves no one will read it. Businessmen take three times as long as professional communicators to say something. There's a real art to distilling a story or article into the bare, readable facts, so the final product needs the hands of a professional in it somewhere, whether he is an employee or outside adviser.

Agency

While it's best to do it all in-house, many companies prefer to have their paper produced by an outside agency. You can always start from small beginnings, with an agency doing the job for you, and gradually wean yourself on to your own operation. As a very rough guide, an out-of-London agency would charge somewhere around £2000 per issue. That would be for an eight-page newspaper, with the agency planning the content, writing the copy, editing, doing the layout and seeing it through the printers. The company's input would be the information, pictorial content and paying for photography and printing.

Contents

It's surprising how much information even a small newspaper contains. Taking 20 industrial journals as examples, ranging from 12 to 20 pages and with circulations varying from a few thousand to hundreds of thousands, here are some typical contents.

Identity

The first thing you notice about an established and successful company magazine is that, as well as having a familiar masthead and a regular size, format and distribution dates, the reader knows where to turn for a particular section. In other words, he knows what to expect on each page. This is an important aspect of newspapers. People *expect* to find their crossword on page 10 and the sport near the back, and only in exceptional circumstances should the mix be altered.

The order of events you choose is fairly immaterial. You can copy a national paper or strike out on your own. The vital thing is that having found a successful recipe you stick to it. Remember, too, that some pages are 'stronger' than others. The front, back and centre pages are very prominent, and right-hand pages tend to get looked at before the left-hand ones. Don't forget, too, that quite a few people read their newspaper from the back!

Front page

This is the obvious page for your most important story – the 'lead'. As a general rule, try not to clutter the front page with too many stories and pictures, especially if you've got a good lead story and an exciting picture to go with it. This is the place for a powerful headline, two or three varied supporting stories, two or three photographs and some 'teaser' information about what goodies you have inside.

You can tell a lot about a newspaper's philosophy from its front page – whether it's written for the benefit of employees or management. By all means show the chairman occasionally, particularly when reporting on financial results, but essentially the front page should be about company *people*, *events* and *news*. Some typical leads taken from a random selection of papers are: new product launched; staff Christmas fair breaks charity record; quick-thinking employee saves factory from fire; product selling like hot cakes; new sports club launched; new pay deal; the annual results.

News stories

This, after all, is why it's called a *newspaper*. The actual news content may only be a small proportion in some cases but it's still the *raison d'etre* of the medium. News means anything from the fact that security guard Arnold Ellison has saved 5000 milk bottle tops, to the sudden death of the managing director. Most items about products, people, trade unions, achievements, failures, pay, appointments, figures and sport are worth reporting. Clearly there comes a cut-off point at which an item is too small for inclusion, but there are no set rules. It will depend on factors like the amount of news available for that issue, how many pages and readers there are, and whether or not the company has newsletters to cater for the run-of-the-mill stuff like retirements and departmental darts results.

Always remember, though, that a long service award or promotion – in fact, any event in someone's life – is *news*, not only to the person concerned, but to his colleagues, family superiors, subordinates, friends and anyone else with any sort of connection with his department or location. That's an awful lot of people.

A newspaper is only as strong as its news *sources*. In addition to your own reporters going out scavenging for information there should be a sound network of contacts or correspondents in each location – in other words employees with an honorary responsibility for keeping tabs on what's going on in their own area. And don't forget the company's own press releases.

Features

If news is the bread, then features are the butter. Relevant and absorbing features will attract people to the publication. A great advantage of features written by outsiders in company newspapers is that they can rarely be accused of bias. It's a fact of life that many employees automatically assume that the *news* in their company paper is management propaganda. But good, interesting features can be both unbiased and readable.

What should you write about? Around the industry – what the competition is up to; departmental focus; personality profile – an in depth interview with a well-known and interesting employee; you and your money; collector's corner; pages from the past; motoring, gardening and DIY. Then there are general interest items on everything from conservation to the European Market. In other words, features should aim to catch the readers' attention and give them something enjoyable and interesting to read. There are dozens of sources in addition to your own editorial team – ranging from the very expensive to those which are free, but watch out for giving manufacturers of pet food and fertiliser too much free advertising space! If you can't find outside professionals to write your general interest columns there's probably at least one employee who's an expert on angling, car maintenance or rose growing who would enjoy the kudos of having a personal column. Almost every professional journalist is interested in freelance work, so why not approach those whose material you like for an occasional feature. The important point is to give your publication an exclusive touch, with some tailor-made comment. Your local MP, for example, will probably be only too happy to contribute from time to time – in return for a bold party political picture with a vote-winning smile!

Editorial

Many company newspapers include a regular editorial comment. Don't feel compelled to have one in yours. There's no reason why you shouldn't write a short comment on some burning issue or other, but it'll create two problems for you: first, it's hard to come out with a punchy, pertinent comment for issue after issue; and second, remember that the editorial leader is the space where a paper nails its colours to the mast and displays its social and political convictions. If you want to write an editorial column, by all means do so – but do it with your eyes open.

One or two papers contain a message from the chairman or chief executive in place of an editorial. This has the advantage of communicating directly from the top person to every employee, but be warned – direct management messages are fine from time to time, but on a regular basis they fuel the propaganda argument and can emasculate the newspaper in its task of trying to identify with readers.

Sport

Sport is an important section of the company newspaper, although less so than the nationals and locals. Unless you have a very sporting company the pages can be hard to fill, and somehow the buying department's 8–0 win over office services doesn't merit quite the same treatment as Manchester United defeating Nottingham Forest.

All the same, it is important material – especially to the participants – and should merit one or two pages in any company paper. Don't feel you have to use the *back* page for sport; that page can be put to better use for some of the livelier stories about the company and its people.

Soccer is usually the favourite sport, but be sure your reporters and correspondents aren't missing out on any of the other sports for which the various departments and locations have teams. Plenty of companies shine at hockey, athletics, judo, shooting, archery, angling, cycling, etc. Nor does it have to be all outdoor, strenuous stuff. Darts, snooker and inter-departmental quizzes are just as important. And don't forget the loners – the runners, walkers, yachtsmen and others who go out and break records without telling anyone.

Photographs are very important on the sports pages. At the very least include some mug-shots of the stars and a few team pictures but, most important, get in plenty of action shots, even if they're only taken by an enthusiastic amateur on the sidelines. Cropping is an important skill in dealing with sports photos; if done properly it can double the action. It's best to delegate one member of your staff to look after the sports section – preferably somebody who's interested in the subject.

Competitions

Competitions such as a crossword or brain teaser in each issue make good participative material, especially if the prizes are worth having. It shouldn't be too difficult to create them and £25 or £50 for the first correct answer received will encourage the entries.

Many other types of competition have been used successfully: photographic (serious, numerous categories, high level of entry, excellent reproduction of winners); holiday snaps (good fun, amateur standard, plenty of smaller prizes); spot the ball; Christmas quiz; spot the difference (use a line drawing for one picture and then paint out a dozen small differences with correcting fluid for the second); name the stars (to whom do these eyes/mouths/hair belong?); and an endless stream of those contests where a list of features have to be placed in the same order as that chosen by the judging panel.

Local and daily newspapers and national magazines will give you plenty of other ideas if you need them. Try to set aside a reasonable budget for prizes and don't forget that many manufacturers will offer sample products for prizes in return for a little publicity.

Fillers

There are plenty of other devices for filling space and encouraging reader interest. These 'shorts' have another function in that they vary the pace of reading. They're the spice in the publication pudding. Again, check your local paper or scan other company newspapers for ideas. Such fillers include special offers (make sure they are special and can't be bought cheaper elsewhere and that they're safe and workable), local events, cinema/TV/radio listings of relevant topics; a 'Did you know?' section; snippets from old publications; plugs for forthcoming events; and special features in the publication itself.

Advertisements

Advertisements are the life-blood of national and local newspapers. Without advertising revenue they wither and die – unless they're privately funded or are designed to operate as a loss leader.

This should never be true of company publications. If a little extra cash can be generated by advertising to offset your costs, well and good, but it must only be seen as a welcome bonus.

Only the very largest private and public organisations will have a large enough readership to justify approaching outside advertisers. A typical example are the car maufacturers whose professional tabloids always carry a large number of display adverts from, yes, car dealers wanting to sell cut-price models to employees. Papers published for the nationwide utilities of coal, gas, electricity – and, more recently, water – will naturally be the place for suppliers to those industries to advertise. But, overall, paid display advertising should not be your concern. If you *do* feel that your readership is big enough to attract an advertiser – say 50 000 readers – then you'll need to compare advertising rates in local newspapers and trade journals, make up your own rate card and run the activity on a professional basis. You may even wish to call in the services of a space-selling agency to take this part of the action out of your busy schedule.

Where advertising can be of real benefit in the company newspaper is in the classified section, those columns of small ads for everything from a time-share in Majorca to a used portable typewriter and a set of 1930s *Encyclopaedia Britannica* (one volume slightly chewed). This is often the most popular page in a publication, particularly when a paper serves a large number of people in one or two locations. Test your market and see what the response is. If numbers are few and locations widely spread, individual site bulletin boards may be a better way of catering for the human acquisitive streak.

Here are a few points to watch out for.

- Always include a cut-out form in each issue and insist on typing or printing in block capitals.
- Insist on home telephone numbers being given (or you'll run into serious trouble with every department manager).
- Run each ad for a fixed number of weeks.
- Include a disclaimer on the quality and value of the goods advertised.
- Print an occasional success story (one in each issue if you can) on how successful the section has been in providing, eg a dream holiday for Bert and Brenda, the remaining copy of *Be Your Own Car Mechanic* for Steve Hackett to complete his set and a loving home for each of Miss Stockley's four Siamese kittens (pedigree supplied).

Photographs

Pictures can make or break a publication. It's fine for the nationals who can choose from hundreds of prints of the Prime Minister, car crashes, soccer violence or film star glamour to lure the reader through their pages.

Most of the pictures that come the way of the company paper, however, are those waxwork portraits of managers trying to look relaxed, groups of dozens of people standing motionless around a retiree, long-service awards and the new grinding machine for the Piddletrenthide plant. That's not to say that these pictures aren't important. They're what the company is all about, and even a dull picture is better than the proverbial thousand words. But it's essential to add some pictorial spice to the publication.

The first question to consider is *who* takes the pictures. Again, there are more sources than you might think. Some larger companies have their own photographic departments, but most firms will have to rely on other sources. For a start, pictures taken for the local paper can be bought and reproduced (with permission) very inexpensively. So it's worth keeping regular contact with the local paper so that you're kept informed of any employee activities such as weddings, lottery prizes, VIP visits to factories, mayoral appointments or sponsored parachute jumps.

For some events it's worth commissioning a good local photographer to do the job for you, so another important point of contact when setting up a company newspaper is a good professional photographer near each of the company's main locations. Ask your local paper to recommend a good freelance *news* photographer. Few *general* photographers understand what looks good on a newspaper page. But you don't always have to go outside the firm. In any group of, say, a thousand people, there's likely to be at least one who makes a serious hobby of photography and has sufficient expertise and equipment to take some really good pictures. So perhaps you can pay one or two employees to act as 'freelance' photographers for the company paper in their spare time. And, of course, there are your own advertising and PR people. Make sure that when they send photographs of company products and personalities to the outside world you get a copy too.

Before a photograph is even taken, don't be afraid to specify what you want. A photographer should have the flair and imagination to do much more than simply line the subjects up and press the shutter. Tell him beforehand what you want in the picture. If it's a retirement or presentation try and get the people involved actually doing something – even if it's only a 'thumbs up'. It's not enough just to stand there shaking hands and half-smiling nervously at the lens. If it's a big building, stress that you want its size and scale to come out in the picture. If it's a product, say which features you want to emphasise. Once you've got the picture in your hands, have a good look to see if there's any more that can be done. How big or small do you want it on the page, and can it be 'cropped' to accentuate the interesting features and cut out the boring ones. An outstanding guide to newspaper photographs is *Pictures on a Page* by Harold Evans, published by Heinemann. Using hundreds of photographs, it explains selection, briefing, what makes a photograph, composition and cropping and is packed with good advice.

Graphics

Photographs are not the only way of illustrating a paper. Drawings have their place, too. They are especially useful for explaining difficult concepts – such as the effects of inflation, or the structure and workings of industrial relations procedures. There are plenty of professional illustrators. Try your local design studios for a start, you may be lucky enough to have a good artist in the company, but in each case it's important to work closely with the illustrator.

Cartoons and comic strips can be another good device for livening up a page and giving the readers something to chuckle over. But they must be good. There are plenty of cartoon agencies and amateur cartoonists, although a high proportion of the latter produce pretty poor results.

What do they want to read?

Later in the book we'll look at the importance of conducting regular surveys among your readers. It's not enough to churn out what *you* think is a great paper. The real task is to produce what *they* want to *read*. In a company newspaper this is essential. One large company was advised by three experts – including two top Fleet Street journalists – to scrap a particular section from its newspaper on the grounds that 'they'll never read that stuff' (it was a quarter page of information on contracts and the progress of rival companies). Yet a thorough survey showed that it was one of the most popular parts of the whole paper. So keep a regular finger on the pulse, and don't be afraid to go round soliciting employees' views for yourself, in addition to carrying out partial and full-scale surveys.

Based on a survey of hundreds of employees in a manufacturing company, here are the eight subjects people most liked to read about (in descending order):

- stories about other employees – successes, retirements, etc;
- news about the company – progress and products;
- news about other companies in the industry;
- classified advertisements;
- cartoons;
- letters;
- sport;
- news about other departments.

Remember that these are only the preferences in *one* company. A similar survey in another firm showed that sport was one of the *least* read sections. There's really no substitute for finding out for yourself.

Layout

It's equally important for a professional touch to be applied to the *layout* of the paper. Designing a page is one of those jobs which looks easy and is in fact extremely difficult. If an amateur does it, it will *look* amateur.

Some successful company newspapers use a professional layout expert from a national or leading provincial paper for one or two days per issue, working closely with the editor either at the company or the printers. Many papers rely on an experienced editor to supervise layout, while others hand that part of the job over to an agency with its own layout staff.

The vital task of good layout involves not only designing the pages and instructing the typesetter, but also a final checking of each page before it's committed to print. You'll usually get poor results if you just leave the whole thing to the printers since good printing is a very precise discipline and too much interpretation will only lead to trouble.

While the final professional touches should be applied by an experienced layout expert, there's every reason for you to be involved in the overall form and impression – after all it's your paper. Again, becoming an 'instant expert' is possible here and the same rules apply – look at all other newspapers constructively and critically, asking yourself which aspects appeal to you and why. It's important for the designer to have a good working relationship with the editor. Be completely honest – say what you like and why, but at the same time don't pretend to be a professional equal, and be prepared to take 'no' for an answer if good reasons are given.

Layout technique takes years of experience and merits a whole book of its own, so this section can only provide a few pointers and describe some of the devices available to you.

Paper

First, there's the quality of *paper* you use. The higher the quality (ie thicker, glossier and whiter), the better the standard of reproduction, especially for photographs. At the same time it becomes very expensive as the quality goes up and you move in style from the instant attraction of a newspaper towards the permanent quality of a magazine. Think also about using recycled paper if that matches your company's corporate image.

Masthead

Then there's the *masthead*, the title which distinguishes one paper from another. Choose carefully, as it's bad policy to change the masthead more than once in a blue moon. The reader likes to recognise the paper.

Headlines

Headlines provide a wealth of variety and appeal. There's everything from front page 'three-deckers' to one-word eye-catchers tucked away in a corner. As a general rule it's best not to con the reader by advertising a nondescript story with banner headlines, but you can be very flexible. Basically, you want to command the reader's attention with one major item on the page, so avoid what are known as 'clashing heads' two headlines of the same size and typeface adjacent to each other. And as a general rule keep them short and punchy.

Subheadings

Nothing is guaranteed to turn the reader off more than acres of unbroken print, so you have to look for ways to break the text into easly-digested packages and entice people to read on. *Subheadings* and one-word 'cross-heads' help to break up the story. So, too, do important passages of text suddenly appearing in larger type, italics or in a bold face.

Typeface

This leads on to the *typeface* itself which, more than anything, will dictate the 'house style' of the whole paper. It will therefore require careful choice. Having selected a particular general typeface, don't be afraid to put some stories – and headlines – into a different one to give the page variety. This is where layout expertise is important because too little variety of typeface will make the page boring and indigestible, while too much variety (a common weakness in local newspapers) will make it look fussy and confused.

Teasers

There are plenty of other devices to keep the reader's appetite whetted, such as *teasers*. These are the headlines and boxes that say things like 'How to improve your Sex Life – see inside'.

Variations

It doesn't all have to be *black-on-white*. It's almost as easy to print parts in white out of black (called a 'WOB') to make certain headlines stand out, or to print in white or black on a grey 'tint' background.

Variety can also be achieved by underlining headlines and separating stories, dividing items with lines or rules of different thicknesses or putting them in *boxes*. If the paper carries *advertisements* they can be used as a layout tool to break up the page. This applies especially to all *graphics* (photographs, drawings, designs, cartoons) which should be mixed with the print to give a good balance.

This only just scratches the surface, but at least it demonstrates one or two of the main devices and how they can be used to make the reader want to pick the paper up and read it.

Golden rules of layout

There are hundreds of different layout 'tools' which you can disover for yourself with a closer scrutiny of your daily reading. There are also plenty of 'dos and dont's' which aren't so eay to work out – hence the need for professional layout people. As a useful reference, however, here are some golden rules.

- **DO** have a definite lead story on every news page. This should dominate every other news story on the page.
- **DO** try to cut down the number of stories per page – seven or eight maximum – if you are tight on space, stories can be 'subbed' down and grouped together in 'news in brief'.
- **DO** pay particular attention to the use and cropping of pictures. The pictures should have as little waste area as possible, and commissioned photographers could be briefed with this in mind. Often *one* picture can tell the story much more effectively than a selection of smaller ones.
- **DO** avoid too many pictures on *news* pages. One good news picture, reproduced large and one or two small ones, provides a better display than a 'patchwork quilt' of pictures.
- **DO** try to avoid clashing headlines: use tone or white on black panels for headlines where necessary.
- **DO** have a definite centre spread of pictures. This should consist of mainly display with little text.
- **DO** try to balance 'heavy' stories and 'light' stories together.
- **DO** use more ornate display typeface for feature stories – especially where linked to pictures.
- **DO** alternate roman and italic display faces. A good combination is italic for left-hand and roman for right-hand page leads. And don't forget to use 'bolder' types.
- **DO** 'colour' pages by alternating bold and light body type – it helps to break up the page.
- **DO** try to start first paragraphs of major stories with bold type.
- **DO** break up copy with sufficient cross-heads.

That gives you plenty to be getting on with. Once you (and the readers) are happy with the style of your layout, then stick with it. Don't chop and change too much. Rather, introduce any changes a bit at a time. Every few years, think about the possibility of a re-launch – a complete re-vamp of the whole paper, possibly even of its shape and size. But remember, this is drastic surgery. Only re-launch a paper when it really is time for a very big change.

Printing

It's one thing to produce a *newsletter* 'in house', but the best people to print *newspapers* are newspaper printers. Fortunately there are hundreds of such companies all over the country, and nearly all of them print dozens of lesser publications in addition to the local papers. Your first job is to check on the printers in your area. Local newspapers will carry the names and addresses of their printers. Consult also the *Yellow Pages*, local trade directories and the membership lists of the British Institute of Printers and the British Association of Industrial Editors (BAIE). Having discovered what printers are within a reasonable distance, you're then in a position to choose the one you want on the basis of quality and cost. Ask their sales managers to give you samples of any similar work they do and get from them a rough estimate of what they'd charge, based on your description of what you want. Make sure, too, that they'll be able to produce your paper on the day you want it, without too many snags.

Once you've selected your printers, spend a day or so with them seeing how publications are produced and meeting some of the key people. There'll be plenty of times when things go wrong and you'll be glad you know who to talk to and what the nature of the problem is. Quite a few printers will allocate a compositor who will then be the regular man on your job. This is useful as you can learn to work effectively together.

Twenty years ago we would have had to take the next couple of pages to discuss whether to use letter-press or litho printers. Now that letter-press or 'hot metal' printers have virtually disappeared from the commercial world you will be dealing with a printer who prints by the litho method in which the impression of the page is 'offset' on to either separate sheets of paper or a continuous roll or 'web'. Web offset is used by all the national printers of magazines and newspapers. It's quicker and cheaper, but you will need a minimum run of perhaps 20 000 copies and more.

DTP or not DTP?

Having discussed printing methods we should also deal with the rapidly growing phenomenon of desk top publishing or DTP. At present DTP has still to prove itself as an origination system for the printed page against the traditional methods of 'cut and paste' but it has scored some notable triumphs already, particularly in the newly-equipped, fully-electronic national newspaper offices.

So far as the average company office user is concerned DTP

means one or more personal computers using word processing and layout software programs, with the output being produced as a single A4 page – ready for the platemaker – on a laser printer.

There are obviously many advantages with the system. The news stories and features can be jiggled around on the computer monitor screen and cut or adjusted to fit, without a single word being set in the conventional way. Proofs of pages can be sent to managers for approval and their comments or changes incorporated within minutes. Software packages can now be bought providing 'instant' artwork which can be incorporated into your pages. Scanners are being developed which can bring the image of photographs and diagrams on your desk into the page on the monitor. A large number of typefaces are available within the software programs and the laser printers themselves.

But whatever the advertisements claim or the company reps say to you in demonstrations, everything in the DTP garden is not rosy.

- The quality of the finished product is not yet up to the quality of phototypesetting – although computer bureaux are now springing up which will take your pages on disc and enhance them to a much greater density.
- To do the job properly you will need to spend a large amount of money and, perhaps more important for the busy manager, a large amount of time in learning the system.
- Setting your own type and designing your own pages is a painstaking task and you will need to have sufficient people to master the process in case of illness or a change of jobs.
- Despite the claims of advertisements, DTP does not change the need to have a good designer.
- The immediate availability of dozens of different typefaces and a bank of assorted shapes, charts and graphic symbols often goes to the editor's head and a worse product emerges than would have been produced by traditional methods.

Despite these caveats, any modern industrial communicator should be familiar with as many branches of information technology as possible and should investigate the pros and cons of DTP for themselves. This is not the place to compare the costs or the merits of IBM versus Mackintosh, or of Ventura Publishing versus Aldus Pagemaker. It is better for you to either go on one of the many courses run by the professional associations and training companies, (eg BAIE, IPR (Institute of Public Relations), PRCA (Public Relations Consultants Association), IABC (International Association of Business Communicators)) or buy some consultancy hours from one of the many DTP specialist consultants now in orbit. Or try, if you can, to talk to someone who has already had the experience of running a company newspaper or magazine on a desk top publishing system.

Further information

The above can only hope to be a very brief guide – giving you an idea of what's involved in producing your own company newspaper and in explaining some of the dos and don'ts. Fortunately there are plenty of good sources of further advice if you decide to go ahead, or if you already have your own paper and want to improve it.

The first point of contact for anything to do with industrial journalism is:

The British Association of Industrial Editors
3 Locks Yard
High Street
Sevenoaks
Kent   TN13 1LT
Tel: 0732 459331

The Association and its regional branches provide a range of services from training programmes to its own monthly *BAIE News*. They will help with contacts for all aspects of producing a company newspaper – agencies, editorial, layout, printing, etc. They also have a useful library of publications.

There are various books and directories available. *Benn's* is probably the best source of details, with names and addresses of organisations such as feature, photographic and cartoon agencies. It can be obtained from:

Business Information Services
PO Box 20
Sovereign Way
Tonbridge
Kent   TN9 1RW
Tel: 0732 364422

Good sources of reference on how to produce a company publication are *The House Journal Handbook*, edited by Peter Jackson (expensive, but well illustrated) and distributed by the Industrial Society, and the BAIE's own looseleaf *Editor's Handbook*. There are four books in the *Pictures on a Page* stable published by Heinemann for the National College for Training Journalists, namely, Newsman's English, Handling Newspaper Text, News Headlines and Newspaper Design.

Distribution

It's remarkably difficult to see that everyone gets a copy of the paper if you are not mailing them direct to employees' homes. If not, within each location the methods available are the same as those for newsletters. Head office has two tasks: to get the right numbers to the locations at the right time, and to check occasionally that distribution in each one is effective.

If the company isn't too big and spread out, distribution to the branches and factories needn't be a problem. A local freight company can easily handle the job, or you can send a company vehicle or hired van round the locations. For a large company with sites all over the UK it means establishing a complicated network to get the right numbers distributed at roughly the same time. It may be best to send batches of the newspaper by air or rail freight to the distant locations, while relying on vans or a road freight company for the closer ones.

It's very important for all employees to receive the paper as near the same time as possible. Those who haven't received it will be justly annoyed at other employees getting information and classified ads before them. A good tip is to allow a full day between printing and receipt of the paper by the individual employee. This caters for any last minute hiccups at the printers, fog, go-slows and other hazards, and leaves plenty of time for the batches to get through to the outposts and be sorted. After all, you don't have to work to last-second deadlines like the dailies, and only very rarely will you miss any important news by printing a bit earlier.

Make sure that the nearby locations don't jump the gun under this system. While the papers are winging their way to Inverness and Cornwall ensure that the Battersea copies are held in security or kept back at the printers.

It's not enough the get the newspapers out to the plants and leave it at that. It's essential for responsible individuals at the locations to be in charge of internal distribution. And keep regular tabs on them to be sure they're doing a proper job of it.

The *frequency* of production and distribution will vary from company to company. A monthly publication is probably the most popular as it strikes a good balance between communicating too little or too often. If the gap between issues is longer than a month the newspaper won't reach people regularly enough to be a familiar item and much of the information will be out of date. There's nothing wrong with producing a paper more frequently, and quite a few companies have fortnightly issues. But frequency brings its own problems. There's a limit to the amount of news and feature material you can glean from even the largest company and it can be a problem to fill the pages. It also costs more, not only in printing costs, but also in the larger numbers of staff needed to retrieve the extra information. The best bet is to start with a monthly issue and come out more frequently once there's enough material. But don't be in a hurry.

Friday is a good day to distribute. It's the end of the working week, and employees are often in a more cheerful mood and can read it over the weekend. But it doesn't matter too much which day you choose. The important thing is that it should come out on the *same* weekday or date in the month each time.

Costs

The cost of running a newspaper can vary enormously depending on how you allocate finances. For example, you have ten factories, each with a voluntary correspondent – an employee who keeps tabs on what's going on in the plant and sends you the information. He does so, perfectly reasonably, in company time. So, is that time – say a couple of hours a week – charged to your cost centre or do you simply not account for it? Certainly, a company newspaper is going to cost a fair bit whatever way you produce it. But for the smaller firm, with only a few locations, using marginal accounting for the many extras, it needn't be prohibitive.

Some companies help to defray production costs by charging a cover price. Two further advantages are claimed for this: it probably gives a more accurate picture of the circulation (there will be little wastage if people have to pay good money for it) and it tends to make people want to read it more once they've bought it. There's also an argument that a paid-for newspaper is seen as less of a propaganda sheet than a free one. However, most companies issue their papers free on the sound basis that a company newspaper is a service to employees. With or without a cover price, a company newspaper is clearly a costly item to run. But when you consider the millions of pounds lost through strikes, poor communications and employees not feeling part of a company, it's not so much a question of 'Can I afford it?' The real question is 'Can I afford *not* to?'

Employee reports

Once a year the company has to add up its sums for the shareholders and financiers so it's a fairly simple step to produce a simpler version of the annual report and accounts, add some items of information which affect the workforce, and send it out to the employees. This makes sense. People who spend their lives working for a company have a right to know what sort of shape it's in and some of its plans for the future. A few pages from the management once a year isn't a lot to ask. The whole exercise need not be expensive and it will pay for itself a thousand times over. Without such an explanation, what may happen is that a handful of employees pick up one or two figures out of context from the press when the results are announced – and confusion reigns.

The press are only interested in the highlights and don't want to be troubled with space-wasting items like the details, important as they are, about how the money is going to be used. So all that the staff might pick up from their daily paper is that their firm made a blockbusting profit of £5 million last year. Then, when the pay rise is only 4 per cent, people start wondering where the rest of the money went and what the chairman had in his suitcase when he went on that business trip to Zurich last month.

The employee report can save much of this trouble – and improve employee understanding of the facts of business life – by showing with a few words and graphics how (a) the Chancellor of the Exchequer extracted £2.5 of those £5 million and (b) most of the rest went into new equipment and a new factory to safeguard the firm's future. Alternatively, if profits were down, much dooms-day talk could be scotched by explaining that things aren't as bad as they look on paper, and by telling employees what the board is doing to put things right. And if things really are bad, isn't it time they were told?

Employee reports have another advantage. City sources say that there's a big demand for them from shareholders who for years haven't been able to understand a word of the annual accounts, but haven't liked to mention it. Apparently some of the requests for employee reports even come from bankers and financial experts! This isn't surprising. Most annual accounts are about as compre-hensible as Einstein's theory on a wet blackboard. Even the people who write them don't understand them sometimes!

But it's important to remember that an employee report is only one exercise in communication. Beware of the attitude that says, 'Right, we've given them their version of the accounts; now they understand everything and we can get on with running the business until the same time next year'. On its own, an employee report is a step forward, but you've no guarantee that it'll be understood – or even read. The material that goes into it should also be given orally – with audio-visual aids. And copies of the full report and accounts should be made available for employees who want to know more and who hope to understand them.

Another problem is that figures may be open to misinterpreta-tion, however clearly explained. Hence the school of management thought (and it's still stronger than many would like to admit) which says 'Don't tell them anything; they'll want more'. While there's no excuse for this attitude, there's still an element of truth in it. Explaining the figures in straightforward terms to the employees *helps* to keep things in perspective, but you'll still be misinterpreted by many.

Some of the recipients of the report are only interested in one figure – the bottom line. This figure is then divided by the number of employees and served up as a wage demand at the annual negotiations. There's also the problem of knowing when to stop. A set of annual accounts can take up 40 or 50 pages for the figures alone. Almost everything in them *could* be relevant and important information for employees, yet if you add lots of explanations to each figure, plus a pile of material about employment prospects and investment plans you'll soon be into 100 pages. Somehow it's got to be kept to a maximum of eight pages if anyone's going to read it.

Then there's the tone of the document. If it's too sterile and consists of lists of figures it'll be way over the heads of most people. On the other hand if it's too simplified it'll appear patronising and will lose its credibility.

As long as these points are kept in mind, there's no reason why a company shouldn't issue some form of employee report. These can range from a full-colour 12-page A4 brochure to 4 pages of black and spot colour as the centre pull-out of the regular tabloid newspaper.

What should go into it

Within the constraints of a few pages, and keeping everything simple and digestible, here are some of the points which should appear in any employee report.

Chairman's statement

At least once a year the top person should tell the troops how the war is going. In any case he's going to make a statement to the shareholders, so why not do the same for the employees.

It needn't be long – indeed, it *shouldn't* be long. All that's required is:

- a brief resumé of the key points of the figures;
- a mention of the year's high and low features with praise where earned, and a sideswipe where deserved;
- a look at the year ahead – investment plans, employment, new products;
- any other special items affecting the company (anniversary year, Queen's Awards, etc).

The main figures

First or second on the list are the figures themselves. The profit and loss statement and the balance sheet are 'musts'. Each need only contain about a dozen items on each side of the equation, for example:

WHAT WE EARNED (PROFIT AND LOSS)			
Sales	£25	million (last year 21.5 m)	
Materials	8.5	m	
Wages, pensions, etc	9.75	m	
Other (services, fuel, etc)	2.25	m	
Depreciation	1.0	m	
Total			**21.5 m**
Profit before tax	3.5	m	(last year 2.85 m)
Tax	1.3	m	
Dividends	0.7	m	
Retained in the business	£1.5	m	(last year 1m)

WHAT WE'RE WORTH (BALANCE SHEET)		
Buildings and equipment	£18.2 m	
Stocks of material	26.6 m	
Cash and money owed to us	21.2 m	
Total	66.0 m	
Less: what we owe	31.0 m	
Total (Net Assets)	**£35 m**	(last year 31.5 m)

Any of the terms which aren't self-explanatory should have brief notes to explain what they mean. These could be in the form of marginal notes or graphics. One firm displays the data like a normal sheet of accounts and adds comic-strip speech bubbles to explain in quotes what the more difficult terms mean. For example, terms like 'profit' and 'loss' are left as they are, but something like 'deferred taxes' would get a bubble saying 'taxes we will probably owe so we've set the amount aside'.

The year's business

As these are the annual report and accounts, there should be some actual report on the year gone by. A summary of the year's highlights provides a setting for the figures and acts as an annual signpost showing where the company has been. If the report carries, say, 20 of the major happenings of the last 12 months, there'll probably be a few that many employees may not have known about and others that may have been forgotten. The market share of the products is valuable information, too. For a big company with a number of locations, it may be appropriate to have a paragraph each about some – or possibly all – of the various factories or divisions.

Where we're going

There should be a look into the future. Crystal balls aren't needed. All that's required is a look at investment plans, product developments, trading conditions, and how all this is likely to affect pay and jobs.

Thus, the sections of the report so far say: 'This is where we are. This is where we've been. This is where we're going.'

Value added

The use of 'value added' in accounts is increasingly becoming the hobby horse of accountants, journalists, managers, politicians and others. It has become as controversial as the original debate about whether or not the earth was flat. This is unfortunate because it has attracted intellectual argument and other forms of confusion to something which should really be quite simple.

'Value added' means the difference between what you paid for your materials and services, and what you got for them. Thus, if your company bought in £10 000 of wood, wire and springs to sell £20 000 worth of mousetraps it *added value* of £10 000. If you then show how this added value was distributed you have a fairer picture of what went on than you get from the usual accounting practices which are full of 'depreciations', 'amortisations', etc.

Many academic white hairs have fallen over the pages that make up a value added statement. For example, the way that two different accountants assess what the wood cost can vary to the tune of several thousand pounds. However, at the end of the day you should still get a decent picture of how the cake was divided in the previous year. In fact, value added is invariably shown as a cake or 'pie chart'. Thus, the value added statement will read:

Value of sales		£20 000
Cost of goods and services:		
Wood, wire, springs, etc	£8 000	
Electricity, gas, etc	£2 000	
		£10 000
Value added		£10 000

Thus, the company, by doing things and making things, added £10 000 worth of value. The 'pie' then shows where that £10 000 went:

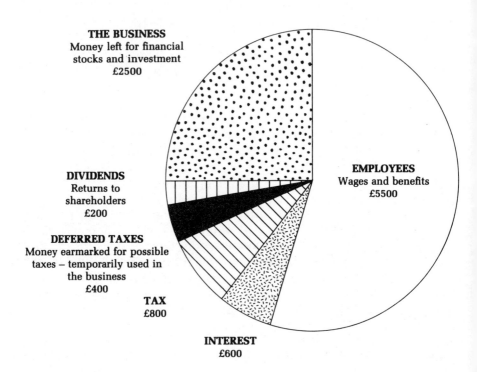

THE BUSINESS
Money left for financial
stocks and investment
£2500

EMPLOYEES
Wages and benefits
£5500

DIVIDENDS
Returns to
shareholders
£200

DEFERRED TAXES
Money earmarked for possible
taxes – temporarily used in
the business
£400

TAX
£800

INTEREST
£600

Employment

The report should also give some facts and figures about the company's employment. This is important information for the people working in it. Did you take on more people? Or lose some? Why? What happened to pay, pensions and other benefits? Were there any changes in personnel policy? How do things look for the year ahead?

Inflation

In these inflationary times there ought to be an explanation of how the figures are distorted by rising prices. Last year's profits might look good if they've risen by 10 per cent, but if national inflation went up by, say, 12 per cent, then you've actually slipped back rather than progressed.

Quite a few firms go in for inflation accounting, or 'CCA' (current cost accounting), and show their results in 'real' terms. This can be conceptually hard to grasp. It's probably just as effective to give one or two specific examples of the ravages of inflation 'two years ago a ton of mousetrap springs cost us £700, last year the same amount cost £1000' and then show what the bottom line looks like both normally and in deflated terms.

Thus the core of an employee report consists of a message from the top person, the main figures – notably the profit and loss statement and the balance sheet – a resumé of the year's business, a look at the future, an explanation of value added, employment details, and a note about inflation when appropriate. There's no limit to the amount of additional information you can include, but there comes a point at which you'll only be writing it for yourself, the directors and maybe one employee in a thousand who's looking for a cure for insomnia. There are, however, two other items worth considering.

The long-term picture

Quite a few firms show not only the results of the past year, but also look at the performance for the last five or ten years. This puts the results of the single year into better perspective and is especially relevant to companies with erratic or cyclical fortunes.

Social report

There's a growing trend for companies to report on what they've contributed to the community each year. This has arisen from pressures by communities, politicians, charities and ecological groups for companies to be better citizens. The social report shows what the company has done to improve the environment by cutting down on smoke and soundproofing noisy factories. It shows how philanthropic it's been towards the needy. And it explains how much it cares for the employee.

Consistency

It's important for the accounting methods to be consistent from one year to the next. Remember that if you adopt current cost accounting one year, for example, you can't flip back to historic accounting when prices drop and hope they won't notice. Someone will.

Graphics

Now for the most important part. As the purpose of an employee report is to simplify the figures for easy digestion, you can't beat pictures for showing where the money came from and where it went. It's tempting to get carried away. Let an imaginative artist loose with a page of figures and you'll end up with cash registers, trains, barrels, cartoons, matchbox men, bags of money and any other device to turn the incomprehensible figures into meaningful pictures. Fine. But be very sure that they *are* meaningful. In the final analysis it's hard to beat old fashioned 'pie charts' and piles of coins or notes. Even a simple table of figures isn't as terrible as many people make out. Some graphics are guilty of being so clever that they become more complex than the original figures. There also comes a point at which the reader's intelligence is insulted.

In addition to pies and money piles, three-dimensional blocks are popular, with the main items of, say, the profit-and-loss account shown in different-coloured bands or bricks in proportionate size to the total block. An ordinary bar chart, for example, is much easier to read in three dimensions.

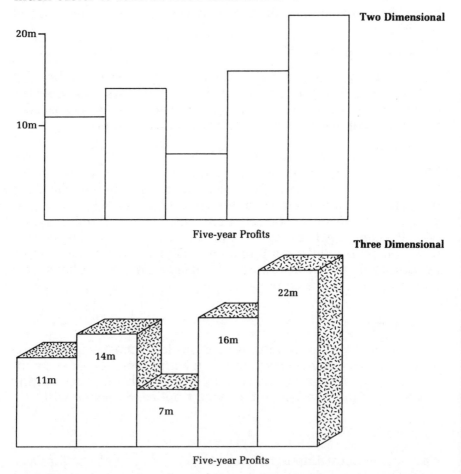

Two Dimensional

Five-year Profits

Three Dimensional

Five-year Profits

The figures shown are the same but it's surprising what a difference a few lines make. And in colour it's even more effective. Similarly, a bit of shading or colour can do wonders for an ordinary *line* graph.

Another popular method is to use pictures of the company's products to demonstrate figures. Thus, a motor company might show its assets in piles of cars, or a builder might show the value added allocated into portions of a house. An old favourite is to show a set of scales with profits or assets on one tray and debits or debts on the other. A small touch like a hand putting the final item on one of the trays adds impact. Cartoons are quite popular, and odd points can be illustrated – and spaces filled – with relevant photographs of products and processes.

Who writes what

Left to the finance department, even the simplest employee report soon fills up with horrors like advance corporation tax or sources and applications of funds. So it's vital for someone responsible for communicating to be involved at an early stage. This could take the form of a PR executive or consultant joining forces with a senior finance person, or letting the editor of the company newspaper loose with a copy of the formal accounts and with advice from a financial expert. The journalistic touch is needed to ensure that the end result stands a chance of being understood.

How to produce it

An employee report can take different forms. Probably the simplest is to incorporate it as part of the company newspaper. This has the advantage of being very cheap to produce. The disadvantages are: (a) it doesn't really stand out as anything special; (b) because of the printing process you may only be able to use colour on half the pages; and (c) on the cheaper grades of paper the colour looks terrible.

The next level up is to print it on a higher quality paper to take full advantage of colour and graphics. This is still fairly cheap, and the report takes on its own identity. It can either be inserted in the company newspaper or issued separately.

Some companies splash out and produce the employee report in magazine form on glossy paper, like the formal report and accounts. These vary from a few pages to massive tomes which are great for flattening cockroaches at ten paces but have few other uses.

Printing will usually be done by the same people who print the company paper, but if you're using heavier paper and colour, or binding it, it's worth shopping around, either on your own, or with the help of a print consultant.

Distribution can be on the same lines as the company newspaper. Some companies send the report to the employees' homes.

Further information

Whether or not you already produce your own employee report, it's a good idea to ask other companies for samples of their versions. They can be a useful source of ideas for (a) what they communicate, (b) how they communicate it, and (c) what they emphasise and what they leave out. Most business organisations (CBI, Industrial Society, BIM, etc) will either have a resident expert in the field, or can put you on to one.

Useful books on the subject include: *A Practical Guide for Employee Reports* by David M Martin (Buddenbrook), *Employee Reports* by Anthony Hilton (Woodhead-Faulkner), *Illustrated Guide to Employee Reports* By Davenport, Elton and Middleton (Industrial Society).

Finally, some consultants in PR and employee communication specialise in the subject of employee reports. But beware of well-meaning experts who give you a laundry list of hundreds of items and tell you to go ahead and communicate them – or who are more interested in winning creative awards than in actually communicating.

Other written communications

Newsletters, company newspapers and magazines and employee reports are the main forms of written communication but are by no means the only ones. Other forms include the following.

Notice boards

Notice boards are one of the most overlooked methods of communication – especially in industry. A company will spend thousands of pounds tarting up its publications to please the eye, while the notice board – which is permanently visible to all – is lucky if it receives five minutes attention a week. With a little effort, a notice board can be made twice as interesting. That way important notices get read.

The first job is to make an individual responsible for it and stress that the task is not only to pin notices on it, but also to keep it smart and readable and to check it regularly and change items when necessary. You will find that it's amazing what you can do with a spot of paint, some decent lettering, photographs, a few strips of coloured paper, one or two big red arrows and some coloured map pins.

Notice boards come in all shapes and sizes. They don't necessarily have to be big wooden boards on the wall. One very effective type is a stand with three or four boards on it like a card stand in a newsagents. This carries a lot more material than a single board and more people can read it at the same time.

One advantage of notice boards is that you can combine social and work information. A notice reminding people to switch the light off when they leave a room is much more likely to be read if it's sited next to an announcement for the forthcoming snooker finals.

Notices in pay packets

It's surprising how often opportunities occur to include a communication with something which has to be given to everyone anyway. Pay packets are a case in point. As each employee has to receive one, or, at least, a PAYE statement, you can often include an important message at no extra cost. It's advisable to be sensitive about this. If every week your pay packet contains a note telling you to work harder you'll soon get fed up. After all, the pay packet is a regular payment for work done and is a 'good news' item. It doesn't want to be soured with negative propaganda. But there are dozens of important items that are appropriate – such as explanations of new pension fund regulations, information about production and product changes, holidays, and thanks from the manager for working through last week's heating breakdown.

Notices in pay packets are effective because you have a captive audience. Everybody opens their pay envelope and looks at the contents.

Briefing notes

One reason that local and middle management fail to pass on items of information from the top is that no one remembers to tell them in the first place. Or if they were told, they'd forgotten it. There's little point in the sales director announcing a new foreign contract or the personnel manager saying that the company must save paper if the message isn't being passed down the line. Regular briefing notes of the 'what's going on' variety provide a discipline – which is always a good thing in communication. Matters of importance are put down on paper at head office and sent to factory managers and department heads. If they then read, file and update these notes they (a) know what's happening in the company and (b) are better equipped to answer employee questions.

Briefing notes are also useful for confirming the company's policies and attitudes on everything from political party levies to equal opportunities. These can be invaluable when dealing with question-and-answer sessions or with the outside world at Rotary Clubs and Women's Institutes. If you don't believe in the need for this, draw up a list of six subjects that have cropped up in recent weeks – product plans, staff changes, dealings with the Commission for Racial Equality, what the firm's local MP said in the House of Commons about imports and the company's attitude to Japanese competition. Then drop in on a few local managers and department heads and find out if they're on the company's wavelength.

When you've recovered from this, start writing. But at the same time don't fall into the trap of communicating for the sake of it. The danger of things like weekly or monthly briefing notes is that in some weeks or months there won't be much to say, in which case you're wasting everybody's time if you contrive something to fill the gap. If it's worth telling, send them a note about it. If not, don't.

Outside media

Finally, don't forget that your own employees read the national and local newspapers. Every time the chairman gives an interview to the press or you put out a release, remember that you're not only talking to customers, shareholders and the public at large; you're also talking to your own workforce. They'll appreciate a favourable mention from time to time.

Chapter 6
Talking

Oldest and best

Oral communication ('talking' for short) is the oldest method of all. Words and pictures go back a few thousand years, and audio-visual technology is only a few years old, but grunts and noises go back to pre-human existence. So, considering how long we've been practising we've still got a long way to go. Maybe it's because we talk all the time that we fail to treat it as an art on its own. How often do we ask ourselves: 'I'm talking, but am I talking *effectively*? Is the message getting through? Is there a better way of saying it?'

Talking differs from writing and audio-visual in a number of ways. The main difference is that in the other forms of communication you work out what you want to say before committing it to the page or screen. But with talking, except in a formal speech, most of the final product is thought up as you go along. This applies particularly to answering questions. If someone writes a letter asking what you are going to do about the faulty heating in the stores, you have to (a) find out that it *is* faulty because you didn't know in the first place, and (b) assess what you're going to do before committing yourself to print. Faced with the same question at a joint works committee meeting you might (a) betray your ignorance of the fault, and (b) commit yourself to something impractical.

Aggravations constantly occur in business and industry because someone misunderstands what somebody else tells them. How many times after something has been messed up have you heard the words: 'But you said ...'? There are several reasons for this. Sometimes words are misheard, sometimes the listener detects an intonation that wasn't intended, and often the speaker accidently conveys something that wasn't really in his mind at all.

These problems aren't exclusive to industry. Many rows between husbands and wives for example, stem from talking. Either one misunderstands the other ('I thought you said *you* were going to put the cat out ...'), or they don't talk enough – or one party talks too much! We may laugh. But if after thousands of years of talking it still leads to divorces or strikes, we're not doing very well at it.

Of course talking has certain advantages over writing. Except in presentations and speeches, it's more informal and natural. It's also more tailored to the requirements of the recipient. You can ask the factory manager a question that's bugging you and – hopefully – get an answer. You can't question a video cassette. And face-to-face both sides see much more of each other's true personalities. It's quicker, too. You can cover more ground talking to someone than you can with an hour of writing or a day of filming. The response to a question is immediate, whereas a written exchange can take days or even weeks.

Perhaps the most important thing about talking is remembering to do it at all. A lot of our troubles are caused by sombody forgetting to tell somebody else. Thus, talking has to be as much a discipline as any other form of communication. We have to remember to talk to people, and 'talking events' like meetings, briefing groups and speeches need to be structured and organised as much as slide shows or company newspapers. All the rules of effective communication apply: simple language, analogies, anecdotes, brevity, and only a few points at a time. If there's a golden rule, it's not to get into the frame of mind of the hardened manager whose philosophy was: 'If all else fails, try talking!'

One rule of communication which is broken all the time is that the *same* person should give both the good news and the bad news. It's human nature for the person in charge to rush and tell everyone when something nice has happened, but to delegate the job to a subordinate if it's not so nice.

Below we will look at some of the methods of talking.

Walking the Job

It's the old principle of 'Captain's rounds', of the boss regularly going round the premises to see that everything's in order and to find out directly from people how they're getting on and what their problems are. It needn't be at a fixed time or date – indeed, it shouldn't be or your visit will be expected and you won't get a representative impression. Nor should it be limited to the chairman or the local manager. There's no reason why the sales director or computer room manager shouldn't get off their backsides every few weeks and see what's happening out there in the real world. And there's equally no reason why it should be restricted to the shop floor. It's just as important for the managing director to drop in on members of middle management or the typing pool as it is to be seen on the production line.

'Walking the job' is communication at its simplest. It's about leaving your desk and *talking* to people. Maybe it's because it's so simple that it seems to be a forgotten art. Managers who will gladly spend several days and thousands of pounds making elaborate video programmes for employees won't devote a couple of hours, at no charge, to going round talking to the recipients of the programmes.

A few years ago, there was a successful company to which industrial relations experts and journalists devoted untold effort to find out why management-worker relationships were so good. Yet it was all made clear when I heard the managing director reproaching the finance director at lunch for not having been round a particular part of the factory for a couple of weeks.

If 'walking the job' is done properly, regularly and sincerely, it's a way of showing employees that you *do* care. It's also one of the best methods for getting feedback from people, for getting a gut feel about them rather than a pile of statistics. But remember those three words: *properly, regularly, sincerely.*

Properly means striking the right balance. Of course, there's a place for formal visits, but a walk round the premises doesn't require a fanfare of trumpets and a phalanx of personal assistants and hitmen. At the other end of the scale you don't, as leader of the team, stroll round the place giving the lads a friendly slap on the back and asking them out for a game of darts. *Regularly* speaks for itself. It needn't be too frequent, and it shouldn't be predictable, but it's an effort that has to be maintained. And if you're *sincere* about it, as with all forms of communication, any initial suspicion will wear off and they'll appreciate your coming round.

It's worth thinking in advance about the sort of things you're looking for. That way you won't have the problem of 'what do I talk about?' This may sound obvious, but only a minority of managers can put their hands on their hearts and say they've recently been round the place to see what's going on.

Admittedly, it has its difficulties. The main one is making time. Managers really are busy people, which is one of the reasons that this sort of contact is often missing. But if it's treated as an integral part of the job – then it becomes less of an irksome chore and more a valuable part of the job.

Another problem can be size. Clearly the chairman of a company employing 30 000 staff in 20 locations can't be expected to make regular personal contact with them all. In fact, though, some top executives in British industry do just that (and one or two make a big fuss of it), but if the top person spends more than, say, 10 per cent of the time on the shopfloor you can't help wondering who's running the company while he's not at his desk. In any unit of up to about a thousand employees it's perfectly feasible for the big chief to be seen by most people fairly regularly, but above that level it becomes more random. However, that's no excuse for not getting round at least some of the people some of the time. And if the other directors and senior managers are doing the same thing, the effect is increased.

Mass meetings

Mass meetings are the equivalent of Monty addressing the Eighth Army. It's less the done thing nowadays for the head of a company to assemble all the employees in the canteen or out on the car park and give them a pep talk. The mass meeting is associated more with shop stewards and loud hailers prior to a strike vote. And therein lies the answer: trade unionists are good public performers. Managers aren't.

If the boss is to address the company en masse he must be up to the task. He must be someone capable of thinking on his feet and speaking convincingly. He must have a powerful voice or know how to use a microphone, which most managers don't. The smaller the company, the easier it is. There's no reason why the managing director of, say, a 100-strong small firm shouldn't get everyone together occasionally to tell them about profits, new orders and major changes. There are two advantages to this. The employees see the top person in the flesh, and there's instant feedback. They can ask him about any points that are bugging them. It becomes more difficult as the company gets bigger. Remember, too, that a mass meeting is a big occasion, so only use it for big news. Acoustics and accommodation are important, too. It's a waste of time if half of them can't hear, or a couple of hundred are crammed together by the door at the back.

In general, mass meetings are one of the least effective forms of communication and need very careful handling. Companies of over, say 1000 employees shouldn't even contemplate it unless the top person is an outstanding orator and your research shows that the employees are in favour of this type of meeting. Nowadays the same purpose is largely filled by the appropriate members of management making formal presentations to large groups of employees which will be dealt with on p. 91.

Meetings of representatives

A common form of communication is for representatives of management and employees to get together round a table and thrash out their difficulties. The most obvious example of this is something like the national negotiating committee of a big company, meeting to fight to the bitter end over the annual wage round.

However, the system has much wider applications, especially at local level. There is more emphasis nowadays on joint works committees (JWCs), where delegated members of factory management and employee representatives meet regularly to discuss every aspect of the running of the factory. In Germany, where industrial relations are generally so good, the JWC system is regarded as a far more important contributor to industrial harmony than the more publicised two-tier board.

An important thing to remember is that they are still only meetings of *representatives*. A lot can be achieved by them but they are no alternative to the direct communication between management and employees which this book is all about.

There are many ways of running JWC's, depending on the size of the works, the nature of the industry, the industrial relations climate and the sort of problems which arise. As an example, here's a description of a highly successful JWC system in one major company in heavy production industry. It has several thousand employees, ranging from a few hundred in one place to well over a thousand in others.

Constitution

At each works the number of representatives on the JWC ranges from 6 to 20, depending on the size of the factory. On a fairly large JWC the management side consists of:

- factory manager;
- industrial relations manager;
- production manager;
- financial controller;
- health and safety officer;
- administration manager (premises, catering, etc).

The union side consists of the works convener and five shop stewards elected to the JWC by all the shop stewards in some cases, and by all the employees in others. The industrial relations manager and a shop steward act as joint secretaries. The minutes are taken by a personnel officer and agreed by both sides before going on record. Surprisingly, despite the often heated nature of the meetings, there is rarely any argument over the minutes – so long as the person taking them is reasonably fast and accurate. In this case the company operates a closed shop so there are no problems over the representatives all being shop stewards.

In partly-unionised companies it would be right for some representatives to be non-union, but this has often led to the breakdown of the JWC. The trouble is that the union members often refuse to accept the non-union members as authorised representatives and the meetings turn into tripartite punch-ups. So the make-up of your employee representation on the JWCs will depend on your company's industrial relations structure.

Regularity

Meetings are held monthly, but can be more frequent or *ad hoc* if necessary. All participants agree that the JWC meeting must be the most important item in the diary. If JWC members delegate too often the meetings lose their continuity and effectiveness.

This is hardest for the management side as they have more outside commitments. In the company concerned, a frequent bone of contention is the fact that the factory manager has had to skip a couple of meetings because of last minute panics, so that important JWC decisions have gone by the board. Sometimes there's no answer to this. But the message is: put JWC meetings in your diary well ahead of time and in great big capital letters and give them top priority.

Agenda

In some factories and offices the agenda can be everything and anything, but they ban discussion of wages and major conditions of employment. There are two reasons for this: first, these subjects are usually outside the authority of the JWC and must be negotiated at national level. Secondly, they are the two hottest potatoes in any management-union discussion and they can tend to dominate practically every meeting at the expense of other important items.

The agenda is usually agreed before each meeting but there's plenty of scope for other business. At any one meeting the two sides might discuss production targets, health, safety, future prospects, car parking facilities, machinery and the food in the canteen. Once an item is agreed on, it's important to report on progress at subsequent JWCs

Departmental meetings

More informally, groups of people involved in the same activity can get together to discuss things. Although they see one another all the time, members of a department soon get out of touch with the company and with each other. Try it out on your own departments at work. Do the individuals in those departments know what the departmental budget is for the year? Are they within that budget or are they overspending? When did they last meet with the department head to talk over any problems? Are there any new faces? If so, what jobs do they do? There's really no excuse for employees not knowing what's happening in their own department, or how the department is doing within the company. But it's a common failing in industry.

It's a chore to take time out for regular departmental meetings, but it's a necessary discipline. Meetings should be monthly at the most (if they're more frequent you tend to run out of things to say and go over the same old gripes). Anything up to quarterly is adequate. Keep them informal. After the department head has run through the main items – such as performance, budget, company activities and staff news – people should be encouraged to ask questions and speak their minds. The aim of each meeting should be to exchange information, spot problems in advance and create a constructive atmosphere. And remember that no one's too important to participate. Communication at the top is just as bad as it is lower down. A departmental meeting isn't supposed to be between the assistant manager and the clerks and secretaries. It should involve all the managers and executives in the department, however elevated they may be.

Team briefings

There was a minor revolution in some parts of industry in the 1970s and 1980s with a communication system called 'briefing groups' – now known as 'team briefings'. This system is an effective way of bringing people closer and getting information down the line. Though the principle is very old (Army 'O Groups', for example), its systematic application to industry, commerce and the public sector was pioneered by The Industrial Society, a bi-partisan body with a council made up of business and union leaders. The Society's aim is 'to develop the full talents and potential of people at work and to increase employee involvement and personal fulfilment through work' – and so help to increase the effectiveness of organisations. The Industrial Society has established programmes with considerable success in many companies. John Garnett, former Director of the Society, explains how it works:

> If people are to give of their best to their work they must know what is happening and why. The reasons behind decisions are the motivators. People do not need to agree with decisions in order to co-operate, but they must know *why*. Profitability and efficiency do not depend upon obtaining obedience; it is necessary to achieve people's co-operation. The difference between co-operation and obedience can be the difference between profit and loss. Communication, and in particular briefing, is a vital part of achieving that co-operation.
>
> The cost of not communicating adequately can be seen in:
>
> 1. Misunderstandings
> About half that goes wrong is due to people not understanding. The other half is due to various reasons including

conflict. In one large company 18 out of the 35 stoppages in a five-year period were due to misunderstandings.

2. The failure to achieve commitment

Briefing will not make boring jobs interesting, but if people know why the quality is so vital and are regularly reminded that their jobs matter, they will do them better.

Example

When a section of a company paid systematic attention to briefing people about their jobs they managed to reduce their total costs by 6 per cent and their processing costs by 20 per cent, because the 400 men concerned became more closely involved in the importance of what each one of them was doing, and understood better how they could individually contribute to the success of the operation.

3. The failure to get people to co-operate with change

Organisations will only get the maximum benefit from change if people can be persuaded to co-operate with the new arrangements. People are naturally afraid of change, as it may adversely affect their own positions and that of their colleagues. They need to be persuaded to co-operate with change.

Example

The repeated failure to achieve the claimed savings when introducing computers is not due to dishonest claims by the manufacturers nor to the incorrect design of hardware or software, but largely to the failure to achieve the co-operation of staff at all levels with the changes involved in having a computer.

Increased productivity, which must automatically involve change for people, is dependent on the ability to persuade individual employees to co-operate with the changes. It is not enough to merely get the agreement of full-time union officials or of shop stewards. It is necessary to get the co-operation of each individual worker who has got to change his ways if 'extra productivity' is to have any practical meaning.

4. The We and They attitude

A major obstacle to co-operation is the We and They attitude, where everything is blamed on 'them'. This is largely a failure of communication, because people have not been told why something has been decided, only that 'they' have decided, or it is top policy. It becomes even more serious within the various levels of management where supervisors so often don't feel part of 'we', because they do not know the reasons behind the policies and decisions they have to pass on. Too often they find themselves having to say to their working group that something is being done because 'they' have decided it ... because it is management policy. In organisations where supervisors are kept informed of the reasons behind decisions they are in a position to say 'we're doing this for the following reasons'. You cannot be 'we' unless you know 'why'.

Team Briefing

A simple checkable routine or drill is required where explanations can be given at each level by the boss of each work group on a regular basis. Subjects briefed in the group are those matters which help people to co-operate. Such a system is known as *Team Briefing*.

A leader will need to set up, at all levels, a tight checkable briefing system, from himself through each level of leadership to everyone in the organisation for whom he is ultimately accountable.

How it works

In setting up the drill the leader will need to:

1. Organise it
— between 4 and 18 in each briefing team
— fewest possible number of steps between top and bottom, ie a team might consist of the manager, his two assistant managers and the level below, so long as the number in the group is less than 18
— there must be no one-to-ones: where, for instance, there are supervisors or managers for each shift or heads of individual units (such as depots), such groups of managers and supervisors will need to be brought together by their common boss in a regular briefing, and not only dealt with individually

2. Duration
— 20–30 minutes
— briefing may be added on to existing management meeting
— 20 minutes spent in explaining the two or three most important points with questions, and 10 minutes for other matters to be raised by those present

3. Frequency
— once a month to all those in charge of others
— once every two months to every individual in the organisation. These are the minimum frequencies. If briefing is done less often management loses some of its credibility. Briefing may be required more often depending on the nature of the business or on additional special occasions. If there is a daily meeting it is probably worth turning one of those meetings, once a week or once a fortnight, into a rather longer briefing. If briefing is carried out every day it is liable not to get done adequately.

4. When

Time will need to be set aside for briefing. At senior levels it will be necessary to put the times into diaries many months ahead, as with board meetings and any other senior management meetings.

— on continuous shift working, companies hold back the shift on overtime to man the job, while the new shift is briefed by its supervisor in normal working time
— on batchwork, between loads or between periods of heavy pressure
— on transport, first thing in the morning or rostered for the weekend
— in shops, opening half an hour late
— in offices, immediately after lunch
— on production lines, before starting up in the afternoon

5. Where

— at a convenient nearby place; in the office, works, or in mess rooms
— it is necessary for someone other than the briefer to man the phone

6. Who

— the immediate leader of the group at each level.

Many managers say that their foreman, charge hand or section leaders in the office would be unable to carry out briefing adequately. Experience has shown that four out of five are able to brief, and by doing so become better leaders of their group. Supervisors do not use the language of senior management when briefing, but talk in the language of their working group. As a result they are often rather better at getting the relevant thoughts and ideas across, thereby achieving the understanding and co-operation required. It is what people receive that matters, not what is transmitted.

7. Subjects

— progress: how is the work group at each level doing? Are we on budget or target? What have been the successes in the month? What have been the complaints and how can we handle them better?
— people: who are the new appointments? What are the lateness or absence figures of the group? Changes in pay and promotion. Fears about people's security
— policies: some item which may have come right through the organisation such as a pay settlement or a reorganisation which affects people in the group but where the decision was taken many levels higher
— points: items that the leader has noted down during the

month which he wishes to stress when he has his group together.

Example
During the month a mistake may have been made by one supervisor which his manager will deal with at the time but will also note in his briefing folder so that, when all the supervisors are together, he can go over the point with them all, thus avoiding the mistake being made many times over.

8. Consistency of explanations
— wherever anything is to be passed on it is compulsory that notes should be taken by the people at the briefing
— where something needs to be passed through a number of levels a brief on one side of paper should be provided.

9. Checking
Like all effective systems there is a need to monitor them — all those who brief will note in their diaries on the day concerned:
— the time the briefing started
— when it finished
— who was absent
— and one-or-two word descriptions of the subjects discussed.
Leaders at all levels can then periodically check diaries to see that the system is working; there is no need for agendas or minutes
— leaders should periodically sit in on team briefings at a lower level
— walking the job a week or two after the reasons for some action have been briefed and asking people why the action is being carried out. Where the answers are not known or are wrong those accountable for briefing can be seen and told to do it again, and helped with how they might do it better.

As is so often the case it is only when senior management show that they care enough to make certain that policies are being carried out that success is achieved.
(From *The Work Challenge* by John Garnett (Kogan Page with the *Industrial Society*, 1988).

Further information on team briefings and other aspects of communication can be obtained from:

The Industrial Society
Peter Runge House
3 Carlton House Terrace
London SW1Y 5DG
Tel: 071 493 8899

A word of warning though, team briefings are a major discipline. They involve a lot of time and effort, especially if it means stopping the line or finishing work early. The other problem is that it's human nature to keep returning to the same old moans and groans. Consequently, some companies set up a briefing system with enormous enthusiasm, only to find that it fizzles out after a few months. After one or two briefings, a section halfway down the chain is simply too pushed that month, so it skips a session. Then another section decides to skip it that month because there isn't enough information or it's all been said in the 'works news'. Other sections start to complain that the ground covered is becoming too repetitive and gradually it all starts to dwindle.

Many companies and communications consultancies now deride team briefings for being 'old hat'. But they have only achieved their reputation for being dated and ineffective because they have seldom been done properly in the first place. If they are handled well – and consistently – they are still one of the best possible means of communication and motivation at work.

The grapevine

The grapevine doesn't really merit a place among communication methods. It's hardly something management can use to convey information in a structured and orderly way. But it can't be ignored, and at least we should look at what it does to employee communication and what should be done because of it.

The most important thing is always to remember it's there. This can be a big help when you're all sitting round the table in another world at head office asking yourselves: 'Do we tell them or don't we?' For nine times out of ten you're kidding yourselves if you think they're not going to find out anyway – or haven't heard it already! Of course some things can be successfully hidden from employees and the outside world. Some things have to be. But for the most part there's not a new product, new supervisor's pay rise, or takeover plan that isn't picked up by someone and passed down the line. And once a titbit of information starts to creep down the grapevine amazing things happen to it.

A fitter walks into the personnel records office and overhears a couple of clerks discussing 'the redundancy in the warehouse'. This, in fact, is no more than a couple of storemen who've been replaced by automatic loading equipment and have been made redundant on good terms. But Fred the fitter makes dark mutterings to his mates about what he's heard and the rumour spreads. Two weeks later a baffled management is confronted by a militant workforce who are on the verge of striking over the closure of the warehouse.

Hence the case for telling people everything anyway. Things are much less exciting when they're imparted officially, and experience shows that often a management will agonise over how to release a sensitive piece of information, only to be amazed at the lack of response when they break the news.

It's the same with the press. If you have to recall a few hundred cases of ginger beer because at a certain temperature the tops blow off, then tell the press at once. That way they'll not be in the least bit interested. But if you try to recall the cases without telling them, and one of the hacks finds out accidentally, you can guarantee a front page exclusive with a screamer headline:

'KILLER BOTTLES COVER-UP SCANDAL SHOCK!'

There are four things to bear in mind about the grapevine.

- It's always there, and it always misinterprets and exaggerates.
- It's therefore better to tell the full and correct facts anyway.
- *Never* try to manipulate it.
- It's only interested in *bad* news.

Ignore anyone who boasts: 'I wanted to get more production out of them so I let it slip that the Japanese were building a rival factory.' It's true that some people do achieve disruption by regularly feeding the grapevine with malicious gossip. But they are usually the people who are close to the 'grapes' in the first place. And if they succeed it's because the grapevine only works negatively. You'll not get anything positive out of it.

Formal presentation

For the most part communication by talking is relatively informal and unplanned. But there's a case for occasionally laying on a formal talk-show to present information. A good example is the annual report and accounts. It's worth going to a lot of trouble to get information of this sort across. The same goes for major events like new products and redundancies.

In addition to briefing groups, meetings, company newspapers, etc there's a firm slot for the General standing on a platform and addressing the troops in person. This differs from mass meetings in that it's more structured, with a back-up of slides or film, and the talk is given to a series of large groups rather than the whole company at once. With a single company location and up to a couple of thousand employees, the chairman or managing director can communicate with everybody in half a dozen sessions. But once you get into larger numbers and several sites it's not so easy.

Here's how one large firm handles its formal presentations: The company employs 30 000 people in 30 locations. Twice a year a presentation is put together. In the spring it's the previous year's figures and in the autumn it might be future product plans, a new negotiating structure or a briefing about the competition. On the day the figures are released to the press, the chairman and a few key directors present the 'package' to the conveners and shop stewards who represent the employees up and down the country. The chairman explains the company's record and position, and the meeting is then thrown open for an hour in which anything goes. The representatives can ask anything they want and honest answers are expected.

The first item is a film or slide show of about 15 minutes, explaining what's happened, and the meeting is backed up by relevant papers and copies of that day's company newspaper containing the main figures. On the next working day at all 30 locations, each factory manager begins a similar operation. The managers have been briefed beforehand at a preview meeting with the chairman and they all have the same package of information. They, in turn, have already added in any relevant information affecting the individual factory. Groups of anything between 20 and 500 people, depending on the size of the factory and the capacity of the canteen, come in for one or two hours of presentation and questioning.

Three important points should be noted.

- There must be some sort of written back-up, even if it's only the company paper, so that employees both hear and read the information.
- It's better for both sides of the meeting if the managers prepare thoroughly for the question-and-answer sessions. The purpose of this is not to cook up evasive answers to potentially embarassing questions, but to ensure that a maximum of questions get a correct and informative answer instead of a lot of 'don't knows' or red herrings.
- It's essential to rehearse the mechanics beforehand to ensure that the show is going to work. Nothing is more guaranteed to make all the hard work fall flat than a collapsing screen, duff projector or inadequate PA system.

There are lots of advantages to this sort of large-scale communication. The main one is that it provides a regular discipline for both sides to get together. It also enables every employee to ask questions if he wants to. And it also means that some of the information gets across. But you're deluding yourself if you think you can stand there spouting facts and figures for half an hour and expect anyone to take it all in. As with communication, the secret is to major on two or three points only.

The main disadvantage is the indirect cost. The actual speaking doesn't cost any more than a few hours of management time but it can be very expensive to take all those people off the job for a couple of hours each. Still, many companies reckon it's worth it and that even more money is saved by keeping all employees in the picture.

A speech on its own, however, is pretty dull stuff. Even sophisticated audiences only register and retain about half the information given in a half-hour peroration. The speaking part of a presentation needs to be supported with good visual aids and interspersed with breaks (eg a question-and-answer session; a different speaker, etc). (For further guidance on preparing and making a speech see *Be Your Own PR Man* by Michael Bland, published by Kogan Page.)

Chapter 7
Audio-Visual Communication

When you *tell* someone something, only part of the message sinks in. When you *show* them something it sinks in a bit more. If you show *and* tell, the message really begins to get home.

Think about it next time you watch the weather forecast on television. Shut your eyes and listen and you'll get a fair idea of how many inches of rain you're in for, but the impact is less than when you're watching at the same time. Also, a long verbal weather report will soon start to flow over your head. Now turn the sound down and look at the pictures. All those graphic raindrops and little circles showing how cold it's going to be tell the story quite well, don't they? It's only when you both look *and* listen that the full horror of tomorrow's weather really gets through!

Now picture yourself on the receiving end of a 40-minute presentation by a manager on the subject of the annual report and accounts:

> 'Gross profits were five million three hundred and sixty-two thousand pounds on an historical basis which gave us an after-tax figure of two million six hundred and forty thousand pounds. This represents an improvement of 18 per cent over the previous year's figure of ... (raises voice above heavy snoring) ...'.

Those figures will be assimilated much better if he shows them at the same time with graphs and displays of the figures the audience recognise, such as piles of coins, objects, weighing machines, pie charts and building blocks.

The grandiose term 'audio-visual communication' or (AV), then, simply means telling and showing.

Advantages of AV

The main systems for employee communication purposes are overhead projectors, slides and video. Flip-charts, blackboards and whiteboards are also useful types of AV. All of these systems can be used individually or in combinations to get messages across more effectively.

Take the waiters and waitresses in a large restaurant: you can tell them about hygienic food handling; you can write to them and put up notices. But imagine how much more they'll take it in when they see a video or even a simple slide show, with pictures of dirty fingernails enlarged several times, shots of bluebottles on an unwashed plate and lurid displays of germs and what they do to your stomach. At the same time you can show examples of how the job itself should and shouldn't be done.

It isn't a magic formula. Audio-visual communication, like its written and spoken counterparts, has its setbacks and has to be kept in perspective. But it does have many plus points, too. Let's look at a few.

Impact

The audio-visual methods of communication come over with much more of a bang. Slides and videos are bound to arouse curiosity, especially in the middle of an otherwise tedious day of factory or office work. So you achieve more interest from the start than you can with simply a rostrum, speaker and flip-charts.

Captive audiences

You can talk to people but you can't make them listen. You can give them reams of interesting material but not make them read it, or put up hundreds of notice boards but not make them stop at one. But when you show a visual programme you have a relatively captive audience. You still can't make someone take it all in, nor are they compelled to believe a word of it, but for all sorts of reasons we tend to want to sit through a visual presentation much more than a lecture or meeting.

Illiteracy

We can easily forgive a works manager who becomes increasingly frustrated at the failure of one section to operate some simple new box-loading equipment, despite the fact that he has clearly had the instructions printed on a large board and screwed to a prominent protection cover. We can equally understand the reluctance of the three men on that machine to say what the problem is. The truth of the matter could be that they can't understand the instructions because they can't read. With our rising social and educational standards it's hard to believe that there are some two million illiterate adults in this country, but it's true. Very roughly, that means that in a factory employing 500 people the chances are that 30 of them can't read. That's not the same as being unintelligent. Or idle. It just means that for one reason or another they can't follow your message when you write it. It's a stroke of bad luck to get three illiterate employees as a group, but statistically all too feasible. The problem on the loading machine can immediately be overcome by the works manager getting the foreman to demonstrate it – in other words *showing* and *telling* how it works.

New products and processes

As well as demonstrating new products, etc. AV is ideal for sneak previews of forthcoming models, planned premises and the like. This makes employees feel much more involved and trusted.

Meet the boss – and Fred

It's all right in a small company where everybody knows everybody. But, as we've seen, you can soon reach a size where a lot of employees never see the chairman, or finance director, or Fred Bloggs in the Lancashire plant for that matter.

Many big companies nowadays use the film or television screen to introduce key personalities and other employees in the company. It can come as a pleasant surprise to Albert in the toolroom to see that Sir Charles is made of flesh and blood, is capable of smiling and has an irritating habit of hissing slightly when he pronounces the word 'systems'. The introduction of personalities needs careful handling, as we'll see later. However, it's a start.

Range

Another plus point for the use of AV is that it greatly adds to your range of communication methods. As we've seen, communication isn't about one single method of transmitting information – it needs a combination of systems tailored to the requirements of your company. The game is changing all the time, and the more systems you can draw from, the better.

Disadvantages of AV

As with everything, there are disadvantages. If AV was perfect we'd be using it all the time. Here are some of the negative aspects.

Cost

AV is a very expensive way of talking to people. When you start putting things on the screen you're invariably talking in four figures – other than for a very modest slide show – and it can soon become five figures.

Unfamiliarity

This is not so much a disadvantage as a gentle warning. A common reaction to being herded into the canteen and seeing projection equipment set up and the windows covered with cardboard is to say 'Hello, now what are they up to?' As with all the other forms of communication, familiarity breeds acceptance, but don't expect people suddenly to be evangelised just because you've spent a few thousand pounds on jazzing up the annual talk show. It'll take time.

Can't accommodate audience

The advantage of not being interrupted is offset by the fact that a prepared programme can't pace itself to the audience. It can't stop and explain a point where there's genuine misunderstanding. Worse still, you're restricted to the same package for a wide variety of audiences. Having made a video on why the company is moving its headquarters from Piccadilly to Crumble-on-the-Wold you then have to show the same story to all levels of employees. However, this situation can be improved on by using slides, film or video as only a part of the total package, as we'll see later.

In the dark

It's unfortunate that you need darkness for many of these systems. The very terms 'communicating' and 'in the dark' are contradictions! Putting the light out introduces an element of impersonality. And, unless you're one of the few with a company cinema, it's a nuisance having to cover up the windows and keep putting the lights on and off.

Getting it right

A printing firm recently gave a demonstration to a group of clients – ironically on the subject of how to use audio-visual communication. First, the managing director got up and took several minutes to explain what the programme was about and introduce the chairman.

The chairman then spoke – haltingly, and reading from his notes – for 20 minutes, explaining in detail what the forthcoming video contained. Eventually he sat down and the lights went out. Nothing happened. It took another ten minutes for them to find what was wrong with the equipment and eventually the show got off the ground. Then you couldn't see the screen properly because it was too big for a TV display and kept shimmering distractingly.

At one end of the scale AV has to be interesting, professionally put together and run smoothly. At the other end of the scale it mustn't be too slick and professional or people simply won't relate it to their own company.

Striking the balance

There is a delicate balance to be struck here. Many of the consultants in the field, if left to their own devices, would go to town and land you with the flashiest equipment, brilliant artwork on the slides, world-famous actors doing the films and top TV talent on the video. Careful now. Apart from the extra cost, is this what your employees really want? Change seats for a minute. Take yourself off a dull sweaty shift, sit in the canteen and look at a programme about how one of your subsidiaries makes automatic banana peelers in Ruislip. Do you really need Sandy Gall or Martyn Lewis to present this? This goes for all aspects of the presentation. It's got to be good in that the equipment must work and the programme must be pacey and interesting. But it's counter-productive if it's too professional.

The received wisdom among communication consultants and AV production companies is that 'employees are used to seeing top quality productions on the television at home, so they expect to see the same at work'. This sounds logical enough but no one has produced any evidence. Indeed, the only practical research to date was conducted among employees of a major motor manufacturer in the 1980s ... and it showed the opposite to be true. There was a high degree of scepticism for company videos using special effects and well-known television interviewers. The employees were no fools. They knew perfectly well that the company had forked out a small fortune on the programme and set up the interviewer with tame questions – so their acceptance of the message was impaired.

Conversely, at a local level, employees welcomed simple, homely productions with the local manager saying his bit and using the video to show what he was talking about (with a few graphics to illustrate figures, shots of defects in badly made cars, etc).

Now the evidence of a single company is not enough to disprove the video (and slide) perfectionists. But until they can come up with hard evidence that high quality productions are essential, treat their claims with a little caution. For example, there can be a big difference in cost between high quality high-band video and lesser quality low-band. Most production companies will tell you that the former is essential. But will your employees really sit there and say 'Look at that, Fred, they've only shot it on low-band'?

Of course, *bad* productions with inept scripts, upside-down slides, problems with the sound, etc will be distracting and counter-productive. There should always be plenty to see, the picture should be clear, the production standards good, and long passages avoided like the plague. But you don't have to compete with *World In Action* to communicate effectively with employees.

Local information

It's important, too, that local information at plant or department level is fed into any presentation which comes from the centre. We'll look at this in more detail with each of the methods.

Any questions?

Another essential is to have some oral back-up for AV. It's simply not enough to shepherd the employees into a room, show them a video and send them back to work. The local boss must be fully clued-up on the subject matter and all the additional local aspects. He should introduce the programme and say what it's for and why it's been done (speaking for not more than four minutes). Then – and most important – he must be there after the show to do something a projector can't do: answer questions.

Written back-up

It is also a good idea, where possible, to have written back-up. Nothing special is required, just a bit of paper showing the salient points of the presentation they've just seen – a useful reminder and reference.

The systems

Overhead projector

Properly used, an overhead projector can be a useful aid to communicating information. It can be seen by quite a large audience; it can be switched on and off with little distraction; and the lights don't have to be dimmed for people to be able to see what's on the screen. It's particularly useful for putting up complicated information – such as flow charts and organisation structures – and talking people through the material.

The main problems are that (a) it is obtrusive, (b) the acetate slides can have a home-made, unprofessional look to them, and (c) few people know how to operate an overhead projector properly; most tend to leave one slide up for ages and turn their back to the audience while rambling interminably about the data on the screen.

The first of these problems is difficult to overcome but good positioning can help. The second is not too serious so long as the slides are at least of a reasonable quality – and a local production company can also make high quality acetates if you wish. And the third can be improved with training.

It is also essential in the case of *all* AV presentations to have a dry run beforehand to iron out any technical problems.

Slides

Whatever the subject – financial results, safety, new plans, new products, new processes – most presentations are much more effective if they are illustrated with slides.

The simplest method (and often the best) is a Kodak Carousel projector and a remote control, preferably the 'magic eye' type that doesn't require a lead. From this you can build up to two projectors. This enables you to 'dissolve' or 'cross fade'. In other words, instead of that distracting flash of blank screen between each slide, one projector fades in as the other fades out, so you move smoothly from slide to slide.

With a synchroniser between the two projectors you can get them to play tricks. For example, let's say you're showing a piece of machinery which has an alarm panel on the controls. When this panel flashes the machine operator has to switch off and get the hell out of it. We've established that showing a slide of that control panel is more informative than describing it verbally. Now, if you're going to use two projectors, you take two photos of the panel, one with the alarm light on and the other with it off. You then programme the synchroniser to switch very quickly from one slide to the other and back again, so that the alarm panel appears to be flashing just like it does in real life. This really helps get the message home. Even though you're only using still slides you're achieving basic animation for a fraction of the cost of making a film. The technique can be applied to hundreds of things: traffic lights changing, a lever being moved, profits going up and down.

From here on you can do more and more as you build up the number of projectors, with several different pictures on the screen at once, and achieve almost total animation and all sorts of other exciting treats. You can programme the synchroniser in advance to do the whole slide show for you – but don't forget that once you've started the show you can't flip back a slide to reiterate something. It becomes like a film – unstoppable.

A spot of cynicism is in order when you get to these levels. Always satisfy yourself that you are the right side of the borderline between effective communication and extravagant horsing around.

Advantages of slides

Slides are worth considering for a number of communication exercises. For a start they complement your basic presentation. It's showing and telling at its simplest and often at its best. It's also cheaper than the other visual systems, especially if you keep it fairly basic. Slides are easy to make and easy to use. Also, and this is a very important point, they're easy to adapt for different locations. For example: the production director of a large canning company arranges for a 20-slide presentation to show changes that are planned for the production line, with details of how they will affect jobs. Different sections of the factory are going to be affected in different ways. So the manager of, say, the label-sticking section can add on or intersperse – very cheaply – another six slides of special interest to his employees. Having made up a show, in the form of a carousel of 25 slides, for example, you can then send the slides on the whole drum round the various locations. All they need to do is to hire a projector for half a day. If you have to get the same message to several locations in a short space of time, you can have duplicate sets of slides made quite inexpensively.

The *back projector* is also useful. This simply projects the slide from behind the screen, giving a good picture in daylight and doing away with the need for projection equipment at the back of the room, with all the attendant hazards like large shadows of heads appearing on the screen and someone accidentally brushing up against the projection stand. You use an ordinary projector and reverse the slides. It has its disadvantages in that you need a special (expensive) screen and it has a restricted viewing angle.

Disadvantages of slides

Slides are well worth considering. However there are caveats: although it's the cheapest method of audio-visual communication, it still costs considerably more than it does for a manager to stand on a platform and speak; it's important, too, for whoever is presenting the script to be synchronised with the slides themselves.

I once attended a slide presentation where the manager read faithfully from his script about production figures and pressed a buzzer when he wanted Joe at the back to change the slides. Unfortunately, either a slide was missing or Joe had accidentally flicked two slides. So throughout the presentation the manager was intoning the script for the slide that the audience had just seen, while a completely unrelated slide appeared on the screen. He came up to me afterwards and said: 'Well, they seemed to understand that all right – they didn't ask any questions'!

At the upper end of the scale the equipment can be a bind, too. The more gimmicks you have the more skilled operators you need – and the more things there are to go wrong. For example, at one marketing seminar, a big VIP audience was to be treated to the latest and greatest in projection techniques. The presentation involved four projectors and over 100 slides, with a pre-set programme involving synchronised animation, cross-fades – the works. It took three technicians a whole morning to set up and after lunch the delegates duly assembled to be knocked for six by this show. The lights went down and the projectors came on. At that moment a technician tripped over a cable and sent the whole lot flying to all points of the compass. It took another hour to scrabble it all back together and was then hopelessly uncoordinated. The occasion unearthed new areas of chaos and confusion.

Synchronised presentations with multiple projectors can be very effective but they must be handled by someone who knows what he's doing.

What goes into a slide programme?

Meanwhile, back on the ground, what should go into a slide programme? For a start, it shouldn't be too long: 15 minutes is ample – with an average of two or three slides a minute. Obviously what slides you use will depend on the subject. All that really matters is that the slides match what you are talking about and act as an aid to illustrate points and make them more effective.

Avoid giving a contrived show, for instance by putting on only vaguely relevant slides. Relate the slides to a script. Start out by writing down what you want to say, then try to fit in slides so that they appear for an absolute maximum of a minute at a time. If you haven't got good, relevant slides for some patches of the text then jiggle the script around a bit. Or make up for it by repeating a key slide if necessary – the title of the programme, say, or your logo. Or make up a 'word slide' showing a few words which highlight what you're saying.

Some people turn the programme on its head and *start* with the slides, then put a script round it. This is actually a good way of doing it because words are a lot more flexible – and cheaper – than transparencies. By this method you start off with a note of the points you want to communicate and then raid the photo library or send someone out with a camera. Only when you've got a programme of the right slides – or at least a fair proportion of them – do you start filling in the words. The big advantage of this method is that you achieve plenty of pace. You only use sufficient words to give each slide a few seconds' exposure. Either method is valid. Why not try it both ways and see which you prefer.

Your draft text for the *first* method (script first, slides later) might look like this:

SCRIPT	SLIDES
Hello, I've asked you here today to show you in advance some of the plans for our new zip fastener factory. As you know, at Zap-Zips we think it's important to keep everyone informed of the developments which will affect your jobs and the company's progress. But I must ask you to treat what I'm going to tell you in complete confidence.	Zap-Zips Logo? -or-Title: 'The New Factory'?
The new factory at Cricklewood will mean more jobs and more promotion prospects and, we hope, more profits. We bought it last year from Slippery Slopes Limited after their profits took a dive, and have spent a quarter of a million pounds refurbishing it. It should be fully operational by next March.	Photo of new factory.
There are several good reasons for expanding at this time. Thanks to excellent team work our profits have doubled in the last two years, and the demand for zip fasteners in Third World countries is booming. The new factory will give us the capacity to make 20 000 new zips a day — that's half as much again as we make at present.	Graph of profits? -or- Crate of zips bound for export?
So who's going to work there and who's staying here? It's very much up to you ...	Recent picture of assembly line workers.

And so on. As you can see, there will have to be some juggling of slides – and probably of the script as well – before you have the programme together, but at least you now have a cohesive presentation with an informative text and relevant slides.

Now for the *second* method (slides first, script later). You start with headings for what you want to say:

- introduction;
- new factory;
- decision to expand;
- employee relocation;
- management team;
- production details;
- housing, shops, etc.

Then you decide on the slides you want to illustrate these points with, and end up with a script facing brief descriptions of the slides thus –

SLIDES	SCRIPT
Picture of new factory manager	The factory Manager will be Joseph Savon, who for the last four years has been Deputy Manager of our Plastic Zip Distribution Centre at Bethnal Green. He is 41, etc ...
Pictures of deputy manager and ops manager (one slide)	He will be supported by ...
New crimping machine	Now, the key feature of the production line at Cricklewood will be a brand new crimping machine which, incidentally, costs ...

And you end up with an equally good presentation.

Now, what about the employees in the zip repair plant at John O'Groats? For a number of reasons they ought to know something about the Cricklewood venture. Some may want to move to London, for example. That material about increased profits and Third World markets is heartening stuff. What's more, you can bet that they've already got their own version of the story up there. More important still, the increased production in London will have benefits for them but they probably don't realise it yet. So at very little extra cost you can send the slides, or duplicates, up to the factory manager there for him to use as the core of his own presentation. He might want to take one or two of the London-based slides out, and he'll almost certainly have a few additional slides of local interest made up so that he can insert his own piece about the John O'Groats scene. That way the local workforce get their own tailor-made version of the main message. It's not unknown for some big companies to make literally dozens of sets of, say, the annual figures and send them out in sets of slides to all the locations for simultaneous presentations.

Professional help

The homespun approach can go horribly wrong and it does take up a lot of time. It's worth spending extra to get expert advice.

AV communication is a boom industry and there is no shortage of consultants who can help in all sorts of ways – from giving you a brief professional consultation right up to running the whole package for you. Nor are they hard to find. There are very few parts of Britain, if any, without at least one AV firm, and the industrial towns are bursting at the seams with them. The following are some places to look:

- *Yellow Pages* (under 'audio-visual equipment', 'film producers', etc);
- Audio and video trade magazines (notably *Audio Visual* magazine);
- Local chamber of commerce;
- PR or marketing departments of big local firms who use AV;
- Advertising agencies;
- PR consultants;
- Your own trade association;
- Business organisations – CBI, Industrial Society, BIM, etc;
- Local university, trade schools, etc;
- Conference organisers.

If possible, shop around and try two or three different firms for their approach to your requirements. There are very few rogues in the business – competition is too fierce for that – but they almost all tend to get carried away. Given half a chance most AV dealers will have you with half a ton of projectors and carousels flashing hundreds of synchronised dissolving slides everywhere – followed by an invoice to match. The name of the game is to get professional assistance but make it clear from the start that you have straight-forward requirements and simple tastes.

As usual it's best to start modestly and build up. You won't cut any ice with the sudden appearances of dozens of projectors, synchron-isers and flashing slides. For the most part, companies who do a lot of communicating tend to use the lavish stuff for the marketing side of things and keep employee communication simple.

Projecting

As long as the equipment is fairly simple you shouldn't need a trained projectionist. It doesn't take long to learn to operate a slide projector, but a specialist is needed once you get into the fancy stuff. The company providing the equipment would be able to help or put you on to someone. A number of bigger firms who use a lot of AV have their own in-house specialists.

It's always a good idea to have a dry run anyway – to make sure the slides are in the right order and that the presenter or projectionist has a marked copy of the script showing exactly where to change slides. Check quietly on the obvious points: does the projector have the right plug for your sockets? And is there a spare bulb? If things break down in the middle of a presentation you can wave goodbye to audience concentration.

Tape-slide

You can also programme in a cassette tape, with any voices you want. The narrator booms out a recording of the script over the speakers and the synchroniser picks up an electronic signal from the tape which tells it when to change slides. As well as a narrator, the tape can include the voices of various directors or company specialists explaining their particular subjects.

Tape-slide has the advantage of giving the show from the horse's mouth. It means that a sewing machine operator in Llanelli hears the sales figures from the sales director, the finances from the finance director, and so on. Each executive can 'introduce' his piece, with a quick mug shot on the slide so that a human being appears where for many employees there was previously just a board room full of 'them'.

Tape-slide can also be a godsend when the presentation is given several times over and the poor old factory manager is losing his voice (he must still be present, though). But always balance that against the fact that a live talk from the factory manager is much more *personal*, however dull.

It doesn't *have* to be synchronised electronically. One plant manager in a big company who has to give the same presentation 18 times on the trot twice a year simply records his talk into a cassette recorder in the office then tells the employees at each sitting: 'The first time I did this, I lost my voice on the tenth occasion, so this is me on the tape and I'm here to deal with any questions or problems afterwards.' Then he switches on the recorder – with an amplifier of course – and changes slides manually at the appropriate moments.

The tape must be of good quality. Use the best equipment you can get or even go into a recording studio which is not expensive.

Making the slides

If you want to keep the costs to an absolute minimum there's nothing to stop you making them yourself. When you buy a 35mm colour positive film for transparencies the development is included in the price. Send the film off for developing and you get back a box of ready-to-show slides. You must buy a mounting kit for putting the slides in permanent protective glass mounts, however. These not only protect the slides but also prevent them warping under the heat of the projector lamp and thus 'popping' out of focus.

Not all the slides are going to be photographs of the works, however. Slides showing graphs, titles, plans, catch-phrases, etc are studio photographs of prepared 'artwork'.

Quite effective slides can be made with only a typewriter and a piece of paper. Simply type the appropriate message on to a page of white paper. (Remember – it's better to have two slides of 10 words each than one slide of 20 words.) The typewriter can also manage simple line-and-bar charts. You can also buy a software kit for producing artwork on an office computer. Prices range from £850 to £1500. For more professional-looking results you can use Letraset for the words and some competent pen work for the graphics.

Then have a local photographic studio take ordinary black-and-white negatives of the result and make them into transparencies and – hey presto – instant slides. Extra effect can be achieved by asking the studio to sandwich some 'blue gel' into the frame so that you end up with white words and figures on a blue background.

One very useful DIY tip: when preparing a presentation it's invaluable to see how the script and slides look before having the professional artwork done. For very little cost you can make provisional artwork slides by buying blank transparencies from a photographic supplier and writing/drawing on them with an ordinary HB pencil.

Doing your own draft artwork has some advantages. For one thing, if you're putting your own work on to the slide you end up with exactly what was in your mind, whereas there can be misunderstandings if an outsider is doing them for you. It's also cheaper, though you must weigh that against your own valuable time taken up in making the slides.

If you're taking communication seriously, and are therefore prepared to spend some money on it, then it's generally best to use professionals to make the slides. There are plenty of firms in the business. If your equipment supplier can't put you in touch with someone, try a local design studio. As well as taking the job of slide-making off your hands they will do a much neater job than you can. Moreover, they have a lot more materials at their disposal to give you a greater variety of colour and design. A basic slide with some simple, computer-generated artwork in two colours will cost around £15. Something more complicated, such as a map or a detailed chart, will cost more like £24 – and you can spend up to £40 for a really impressive slide. A photograph slide will cost around £3, double that if a rostrum camera is required, and 'dupes' (duplicate slides) are about £3 each (coming down to around £1.50 for bulk orders).

It's very important to discuss costs *beforehand*. Many a love affair between company and studio has terminated suddenly because slides were ordered without costs being discussed. The company manager thinks he's been ripped off while the designer is put out by such ingratitude and lack of understanding of the high price of creative work and materials. You can often make a big difference to the bill by modifying your requirements. Do you really need five different colours for last year's losses? Can't that plan of the new toilets be simplified?

If you simply give the designer your instructions he'll usually do as he's told, and no-one can blame him. If you prepare the show together he'll tailor-make the material to your requirements and help you save on the bill.

Lastly, be sure to number the slides – with a small adhesive sticker on the corner of the frame, for example. This ensures that you keep them in order and that they are the right way round.

Time and money spent in preparing an effective slide-presentation is well invested. Some media are cheaper and others have more pace and impact, but slides have the optimum combination of interest value versus cost.

Video

Although the first-ever film was an industrial one (workers leaving the Lumière factory), 'industrial film' is a relatively new phenomenon. Training films were the first on the scene and then, well into the 1960s, it started to occur to some forward-thinking managements to make films for employee communication purposes. Just as several big companies were being evangelised by this amazing new way of communicating, along came the video, which offered greater flexibility, shorter production times and lower costs. For a while the battle raged between the two media. The newcomer, video, had two major disadvantages: it couldn't be projected on to large screens; and if you shot on video you got very poor reproduction if you transferred to film. So, while film was diabolically expensive, very inflexible and took an eternity to produce, it was still popular because it could be shown to large audiences and could transfer to video quickly and cheaply without losing quality. So much for the history lesson. By and large, the quality of video filming and projection is now good enough to be acceptable in most cases, so very few companies still use film for employee communications.

Advantages of video

The main advantages of using video to communicate with employees are as follows.

- It is entertaining and *watchable*. People are more inclined to want to watch a video than other media – partly because they are used to being entertained by the TV screen at home and partly because you can make a video production so much more interesting.
- Video can be used to *show* so many things that are otherwise hard to describe or which are lifeless in still photographs: figures, products, processes and – very importantly – people, not just the management but also other employees in different jobs, departments and locations.
- It is a very *flexible* medium. All sorts of footage can be brought together and edited into a programme. Local material can be added on – or even interspersed. Production times can be short.

Disadvantages of video

- The main disadvantage is one of *cost*. The ball-park figure for a good quality production is around £1000 a minute. Even a 'cheap' production will be in the range of thousands of pounds.
- It is also a medium which is still best suited to the *small screen*. Thanks to technology, it is getting better all the time for larger audiences, but it is at its most effective when shown to small groups. This can be a logistical headache for companies with large numbers of employees.

Approach

There are many different ways of producing and using video for employee communication. Here are some points to bear in mind.

Some sort of script is essential. If you just 'shoot and hope' the result will always be a mess. A 'script' can range from a word-for-word text of the whole production to a general set of instructions and points to be covered. This is particularly true for, say, interviews with relevant managers, where pre-scripting will almost always produce a stilted result. Any material where there is a presenter or 'voice-over' (where you are watching something on screen and a commentator is talking about it) must have a really good script.

This is the area where most industrial videos start to go wrong because the script is produced at a word processor by a writer who hasn't the least idea of how to write a spoken script. Many of them don't even read it aloud to see if it sounds right. So you end up with monstrosities of PR-speak like:

X is a nationally known and highly respected company with a powerful track record of customers, both large and small. Once retained, X tends to remain their suppliers.

That's a real example. It looks OK on paper (well, fairly OK), but it's impossible to make it sound natural when presented to the camera. Sadly, many production companies and clients spend too much time and money on technical quality and far too little on getting the script right in the first place. It's a classic example of using elaborate sauces to hide dull food.

You may wish to use a presenter, but if so ask yourself why. Production companies argue that employees relate to a well-known face from behind the TV screen, the most popular being newscasters and *Tomorrow's World* types. But do they? There's equally a danger that they will feel patronised by the management obviously paying for an outsider to talk to them in simplistic language. Worse, they may decide not to believe what they're being told. It's very much a case of horses for courses. Some companies are satisfied that by using the same presenter all the time he becomes something of a trusted friend to the employees – though to our knowledge none have produced survey results to support this belief.

Others prefer the anonymous voice-over. You have a voice to describe what's going on, but you don't actually see the person behind the voice. This is still acceptable to the 'professionals' as it's a style that many TV programmes adopt. And there's less danger of employees feeling hoodwinked or patronised.

Then there are the passages where relevant directors and top managers explain their material and/or views. Here it is essential that they should be interviewed rather than presenting to camera – for two good reasons. First, most non-professionals make a complete botch of presenting to camera. And if anyone suggests using Autocue (the invisible moving script in front of the cameras – as used by newscasters) try very hard to dissuade them. It is invariably a disaster. Secondly, television audiences have learned over the years to accept *professionals* (newscasters, presenters, weather forecasters) who are looking into the camera, but they assume that *amateurs* looking into the camera are trying to sell us something. Party political broadcasters might learn from this message. We give more credence to someone who is talking away from us – to an interviewer who is there to ask questions on our behalf.

Again, many companies choose to have their top brass interviewed by a famous TV interviewer, who appears in the video with them. It is unlikely that this achieves much credibility, especially if the questions are nice easy ones dreamed up by the PR department. You will probably get better results with either (a) a tough, down-to-earth interviewer asking searching questions which put the management to the test and express some of the employees' own cynicism, or (b) the interviewee simply talking to an invisible interviewer. Although the interviewer is neither seen nor heard in the video, this approach can achieve high credibility ratings. Where applicable, it can be useful to have some *vox pops* from employees themselves. Some productions use questions posed by real employees as the basis of the management interviews.

By now you should be thinking about which production company you want to make the video. It's hard to offer advice here as the right company and approach will vary according to your circumstances. Some companies are happiest with a big, expensive, high-quality production house; others are better suited to the gifted individual who pulls together a few chums and does all the scripting, interviewing, commentary and editing himself. If you have already seen examples of other companies' videos that you like, then it is best to ask for word-of-mouth recommendations. Or you can approach the industrial video makers' trade body for suggestions:

International Visual Communications Association (ICVA)
Bolsover House
5–6 Clipstone Street
London W1P 7EB
Tel: 071 580 0962

Ideally, visit more than one production company and get them to introduce themselves and show their wares. Human chemistry is often as important as technical quality.

Having chosen a company to make your video your role in a successful product is only just beginning! You must be absolutely clear about who you are communicating with and what you want to communicate.

Briefing

The more thoroughly you collect your thoughts and prepare a thorough brief, the better your chances of success. We asked Infovision Ltd, one of the top video production houses, to list the points they would expect to see in a good brief.

The questions that need to be answered are basically:

- who?
- what?

- how?
- when?
- where?

Identifying the audience

Who are we talking to? The first consideration is the audience. Who will be addressed, what are their preconceptions, how do we anticipate they will react to the information and how do we *want* them to react to the information they will be given? It is essential to ensure that the tone and the level are right for the intended audience.

Establishing objectives

What do we want to tell them? What are the principal messages that need to be communicated? Are there any underlying ones that can also be included without diluting the main objectives?

The style

How do we want to tell them? Bearing in mind the audience and the objectives – what approach should be adopted? The choice is limitless. Would comedy be appropriate? Or drama, documentary, investigative, and what about the choice of a professional presenter, etc?

Usage

When and where do we want to tell them? When all these parameters have been considered, it is essential to consider how the information will be imparted to the target audience. In the case of the video for example, the objectives will only be fully achieved if we consider *how* it will be shown. For example, will it be sent out to individuals to watch on their own? Will a presenter introduce it to organised gatherings? Will it be accompanied by printed material? If there is no back-up, viewers will be left to draw their own conclusions or, even worse, with no answers to their questions. Back-up in the form of a presenter, or the printed word must be considered at this stage or the video will need to provide all the answers to all of the questions and, more often than not, this is impossible.

Once the briefing document has been drawn up, the question as to which communication medium to use should be asked. Will video achieve the objectives best, or will some other form of AV do the job better? Maybe a conference should be considered instead?

Once all the answers to all the questions are found, it is now time to consider *which* production company/marketing services company/consultancy to approach.

The role of the sponsor

The role of the sponsor is crucial both before and after selection of the communication company. Having drawn up the briefing document and selected the appropriate communication company, the sponsor will then need to brief producers and scriptwriters.

But that is not all. Sponsors cannot expect to appoint a company, brief the producers and then have little or no involvement. The best communication happens when the sponsor becomes part of the production team. The communication company must have access to the client in order to avoid expensive re-shoots, re-edits, re-scripting, etc so he should keep in touch throughout production.

Working with the production company

It really is best when it's a team effort ... but do try to tread the fine line between involvement and meddling! Many client companies ruin a good production by imposing their own unworkable scripts, too many facts and figures, impractical deadlines, etc. You will also need a good understanding with the production company when deciding on technical quality. You certainly need to avoid a production that looks like a DIY effort – but too many companies go overboard for ultra high quality with thousands of pounds worth of special effects.

Incidentally, it is technically possible to make your own videos – and some organisations do. But it will require a considerable investment in equipment and expertise. And video production is an area well suited to buying services *ad hoc*, so most companies prefer to use outside production houses.

Training

Increasingly, companies are having the foresight to train executives for television appearances. This can be invaluable both for em-ployee videos and broadcast TV and radio appearances. The usual objection to such training is that it might make the executive appear 'too smooth', but this is seldom a problem. A good trainer knows how to get the best out of a top manager without impairing his natural personality. Indeed, training often helps people who may appear stilted and boring 'on the box' to project their true, lively personality. For further advice on training, consult *Promoting Yourself on Television and Radio* by Michael Bland (Kogan Page).

The programme

Video is a thoroughly versatile medium and can be used for most things from a five-minute chat to a feature film.

A typical low budget programme might be the sales manager and manufacturing manager of, say, a paint company, making a cassette about the latest colour range to keep employees in a dozen locations up to date with the products. The programme starts with the company logo and, optionally, some backing music. The picture mixes into a title for a few seconds, followed by the sales manager in his office, with his name and position on a caption at the bottom of the screen. He explains the need for the company to stay ahead of the game with new exciting colours. The screen now shows some of the finished products on his desk and he describes their uses. Then the production manager explains from his office what changes will be involved in making the new paints. 'Stills' of different processes are made from photographs, and some of the alterations are shown by simple, animated diagrams. The viewer is taken backwards and forwards between the managers a couple of times as they explain how jobs will be affected and how the paints are expected to benefit the company.

The whole programme need last no more than ten minutes. Using only the two office locations, with photographs and a couple of charts, the production need not cost more than £5000 which is worth every penny if it means a few thousand employees being kept in the picture and appreciating the effort, although some account must also be taken of the executive time involved in making the production. The company might think it worth giving a fuller account, with film of the machinery at work and some vox pop interviews. Perhaps by now the chairman wants his mug on the screen, and some artwork is also required, not to mention outside film of the new paint being slapped on a house. To this 'core' programme from HQ, the individual locations can easily add their own locally-shot material by bringing in a video company to make their part of the tape. This is a major advantage of video.

This sort of treatment can also apply to presenting the annual figures, explaining a merger, warning of redundancies or simply keeping people in touch with some aspect of the company.

Every year there are further advances in computer graphics and special effects. Used properly, they can enhance the impact and clarity of your programme. But don't let the producers get carried away.

One major problem that most companies run into when making a video is length. So much to say, so little time to say it! This is where the communications experts must have the last word over top management, each of whom will think it vital to communicate dozens of facts and figures, with a rambling peroration from the Chairman and a decree that every word is too precious to be excised. However, experience shows that twenty minutes is the absolute maximum period for which you can hope to hold attention. Fifteen minutes is better. Ten to twelve minutes is optimum, ... and there's no reason why it can't be as short as four or five minutes. Much will depend on the amount that has to be communicated, the nature of the material and the percentage of interesting footage. But as a general rule, keep it as short as possible.

One small point worth considering: no one has ever researched the effect of different types of music to accompany employee videos. As a result, all the background music sounds virtually the same – an overdramatic piece to accompany the opening titles, followed by the kind of muzak that you hear in hotels and department stores. There's no evidence that music is necessary at all; it's added to a video because ... well, because it always has been. If you must have music, at least try to choose something interesting and relevant.

Showing the video

Here's a true story that the author experienced as recently as the late 1980s: I was asked to train the managing director of a major, modern and world-famous industrial company which was about to make a video for employees to explain the importance and consequences of recent management changes. He had made one bumbling appearance on television and they were anxious to put some more life into it. The company had already decided on its approach. They were going to put a video camera on the MD, who would look into it and explain the changes, supported by a turgid written script in front of him. Add a few shots of the factories, a couple of graphs and – hey presto – employee communications!

The need for the video was paramount as the management changes were causing considerable anxiety throughout the company. And the idea of showing the MD was just right. He was a dynamic, down-to-earth, immensely likeable man whose heart was in turning the company round – to the benefit of all employees. And he was a quick learner, so the training was no problem.

The company soon accepted my suggestion that he should be interviewed by a tough interviewer, using a very broad-brush 'script' (ie an idea of the type of questioning and some thoughts as to the most succinct way of answering them). The result was excellent. The interviews really crackled, and a good production company was called in to shoot plenty of 'cutaway' footage of new products and processes. Then came the showing. The company's 'plan' to use video to communicate with its many thousands of employees was to send a copy of the video to each factory and overseas subsidiary. Full stop.

So, the employees' introduction to video was to be called out of their offices and off the production line to be a shown a one-off video of a boss they'd never seen – and then sent straight back to work. All this was assuming that the local video equipment was able to show the VHS format and that enough of the foreign staff spoke English to be able to explain it to their colleagues (a third of the Australian company spoke only Vietnamese, for example!). And there were no plans to make any further videos.

The moral of this sad tale, which is representative of all too many companies, is that it's important to make the right sort of video in the first place ... but making it is only the beginning. The showing method will vary from company to company, but it must be properly structured and well thought through. Group size is important. Small groups of up to about 20 people can watch a normal TV monitor. This is ideal for intimacy and for everyone to have a chance to ask questions, but it presents a big logistical problem in large companies. Nevertheless, many of the best communicators stick rigidly to small group sizes because of these advantages, even though it means making hundreds of copies of the video (not an expensive process) and hiring or buying a large number of players and monitors. Others show to large groups in the canteen or company cinema, in which case, of course, a large projector is needed. As there is inevitably some loss of picture quality it may be worth thinking of shooting and projecting on film if you only deal in large audiences.

Check that they can show your video format. Most companies operate on VHS, but many outposts only have a U-matic player! And do they tell head office that they've only got a U-matic player and please would they send a U-matic copy? Most unlikely! The VHS tape goes in the manager's drawer and never sees the light of day again.

It's also important to remember that video should not be shown in isolation. It should always be part of a package where the local manager briefly introduces the subject and explains why the programme is being shown. After they have seen it, employees must have an opportunity to ask questions and discuss the implications. This needs to be carefully planned by the manager concerned as discussion usually needs to be stimulated. 'Any questions? ... right, thank you, back to work then' is not communicating.

Occasionally the video should be followed up by a survey to assess its effectiveness (see Chapter 10). If you're going to spend all that money on making and showing a video you may as well check that it's doing the job.

Managers must, of course, report any feedback on the sessions. The centre should be told of reactions, questions and concerns. Ideally, each departmental and local manager should receive his copy of the video in a package containing a letter from the boss, briefing notes about showing it to employees, 'Q&A' guidelines (ie answers to likely questions – and perhaps some questions to ask them in order to get a debate going). The package should also contain a set of handouts, so that each employee both sees the information on the screen and can then *read* the relevant data at his leisure. These handouts can range from the elaborate (eg the employee report with the annual R&A video) to a page of the relevant graphs and figures.

Finally, members of top management and those responsible for employee communication should actually go to see a few of the showings in action. It can be quite a revelation! So, too, should the production company, many of whom live in an unreal world and have never actually seen what happens to their precious productions and 'personal statements' at shopfloor level. For video must be kept in perspective. It is a useful communications tool, no more. Far too often, a company dabbles in video and likes the results, and employees appreciate the novelty and take in some of the message. So before you can say 'Twentieth Century Fox' there are more programmes circulating round the company than at the Cannes Film Festival. It soon becomes communication for its own sake. Large amounts of money are spent making dazzling productions about nothing much, not to mention the cost of taking employees out of the offices and factories to see them.

It's essential to have something to communicate in the first place. If you've something important to say, fine. If so, video might be just the tool you want. But before you start, just ask yourself: 'Why am I making this video?' It sounds elementary, but you'd be amazed how many people forget to ask it. Having said that, a one-off video can be counter-productive as employees then see it as yet another management flash in the pan. They should be shown at least once a year (annual report time is ideal), with two to four a year being a good number.

Watch out, too, for new developments and see if they could apply to your company. For example, interactive video, though still used mainly for training purposes, is starting to be used more for employee communication.

Some of the multinational giants now have their own live television networks. With the increase in satellite usage and a relative decrease in capital costs for studio equipment, etc., it's feasible to run your own studio for up-to-the-minute news and developments, including pep talks from the big bosses, and to screen programmes out to television sets in all the offices and factories.

Costs

As mentioned above, £1000 a minute is a very rough ball-park figure – but it can vary enormously according to the format you use, how many cameras, interviewers and presenters you have, outside filming, and the amount and quality of the graphics. It's quite easy to spend more than £30 000 on a 15 minute video, which for a big company showing a really good production could be money well spent. Conversely, we've seen some excellent videos made by a small 'bucket shop' production team and one camera which cost only £8000. Discuss your budget with the production company and watch for the many hidden extras that creep in. Most times, the cost of making and showing a video will be about 50 per cent more than budgetted.

Do's and don'ts

Here are some of the main do's and don'ts when using video for employee communication.

Do

- Keep it in perspective. It's just a useful tool.
- Budget realistically.
- Prepare a thorough brief.
- Invest in a good script.
- Work closely with the production company.
- Keep it short.
- Show the video as part of a communications package.
- Follow up with research.

Don't

- Overrate the effectiveness of video.
- Use it too much, or be too elaborate.
- Use it in isolation.
- Patronise your audience.
- Let managers use Autocue or talk into the camera.
- Take the advice of the production company as gospel (but don't ignore it either).
- Let top management dictate the programme and content.
- Get carried away.

Chapter 8
Getting it Together

As we've seen, written, verbal and audio-visual communications are very different ways of getting information across. There are big differences in costs, lead times and audience receptiveness. And within each of the categories there are several different systems. So you have an impressive array of tools to do various jobs – just like a set of household tools. If you want to fit a plug to the bedside light you don't simply plunge your hand into the box and produce the hammer.

The same is true of communication. Some media work better for certain messages than for others. Take a sincere message from the MD of the 'we've got to pull together' variety. In the company newspaper it may or may not be read depending to some extent on the prominence it's given. In a plant newsletter it would be lost, and on slides it would be hopeless. But shown on video to a small group – the message would come over much more effectively because some of the personality and sincerity of the person giving the message would come through. At that stage, if their attention is grabbed by the video, the message could be usefully reinforced in the company newspaper.

Conversely, a page of queries and complaints from employees – with the appropriate management answers – is best placed in the company newspaper, while a detailed question-and-answer session on local matters would be better handled at a joint works committee or at a briefing group.

Therefore, as simple as it sounds, the first thing is to establish what you want to say in the first place. Then have a look through the tool box for the right equipment. It's useful to chart what methods you have at your disposal and see how they work for different types of information. Your chart can show the methods based on the information, thus:

Information	Methods
Message from top management	Video (small groups)
	Newspaper
Results of pay negotiations	Information bulletins
	Newspaper
	Notice boards
Financial results	Employee report
	Slides
	Film
	Video

And so on. You're not restricted to using one method only. Indeed, the planned (not random) use of a number of media can greatly enhance the effectiveness with which the message is communicated. There are no hard-and-fast rules, just general principles. And, of course, cost comes into the equation.

For example, say you want to acquaint employees with the latest product. An ideal medium is the company newspaper. The product can be given plenty of prominence, pictures and diagrams at no extra cost. For a little extra the pictures can be in colour. You can devote a lot of space to describing what it does, who will make it and how. Most employees will see it and the most interested ones can read it more thoroughly at their leisure.

If it's important enough – and you have the budget – the product and process can be shown on video. This has more impact and shows the product at work. On its own, though, video is only second best to the newspaper, partly because of the much higher cost, partly because you have to take people off the line to acquaint them with it, and largely because they only see it once, for a few minutes. But show it on video and in the company newspaper, and the combination will be more effective than either method on its own.

This leads to the whole question of communications strategy. Rather than relying on communication just happening, it does no harm for the managers involved in company communication to sit down once or twice a year and decide what they want to communicate and how they propose to do it. It's also good sense to have a 'core' strategy – a code of the communication principles for your particular company.

Each year or half year – or whenever you have something major to communicate – you put your heads together for a look ahead. Many of the things that will need to be communicated are known about well in advance. Some examples are annual pay negotiations, product changes, new stores, offices or factories, financial results, major purchases and deliveries, new regulations. For each item you need to establish *how* it's to be communicated, *who* is going to do it, what *lead times* are required and *how much* you're likely to spend on it. This is a simple procedure which is applied to most other areas of business, but which often fails to be used for communication.

But it's equally important to remain flexible within the strategy. Keeping people informed is an art as well as a science. What's more, many of the things which have to be communicated crop up unexpectedly. When the premises department suddenly announce that they're going to turn the heating off for two weeks on 3 January, it's advisable to tell the employees even though it wasn't part of the communication strategy!

Chapter 9
Two-Way Traffic

Let's begin with a little experiment. Find a manager, supervisor, husband, wife or managing director with a few minutes to spare. Sit them down with paper and pencil and *with your back to them* ask them to draw the figure below from your description *but* you must not use your hands and they cannot ask questions. Compare their result with the original.

Here is a series of six rectangles. All are the same size and in each the long side is twice the short side. They all touch at corners or midway along a side. All angles are either 45 degrees or 90 degrees. Remember. No questions. No signs. Voice only.

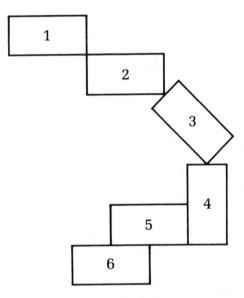

Now do the same with the second diagram but this time face the sketcher. They can ask questions and you may also use your hands to indicate size or direction.

Now compare the results. Although the second diagram is more complicated than the first, it's probable that you will have transmitted it more accurately and possibly more quickly.

So what? Well doesn't this indicate that one type of communication (voice) is improved when a second (gesture) is added? More important, there is a noticeable improvement when the communication system becomes *two-way*. You may say 'Well, that's just

Here is a series of squares and circles. All are of the same size; the diameter of the circle being equal to the side of the square. They all touch at corners or midway along sides or diameters. All angles formed by the squares are either 45 degrees or 90 degrees. Nothing is irregular. Use voice, questions, signs.

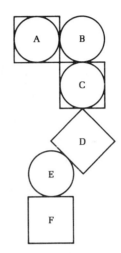

common sense.' Of course – so is all good communication. That doesn't make it any less important. If only we could build this two-way communication system, this two-way traffic, into our working life.

So often we are working in these conditions:

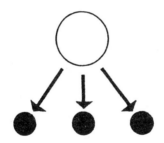

or these:

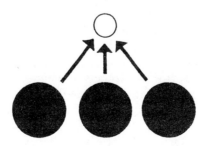

While we should be aiming for this state of affairs:

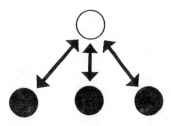

Or, even better, this eternal triangle where information flows not only up and down but across. Links between head and hands are vital but are immeasurably improved when each hand knows what the other one is doing.

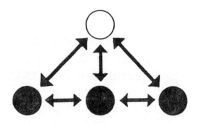

Overcrowding on the up line

How different from our own company, you say. Yes, indeed. Let's face it, employee communication is usually something of a one-way affair. We've looked so far at how to get information down the line from management to the individual employee. That's fairly logical. For one thing, the management has more to communicate. In the course of a year they might want to relay information on everything from the monthly financial figures to the name of the new security guard. And what they have to communicate is often complex – a value added statement or an explanation of how the new pension scheme works takes a lot of communicating.

So most of the communication resources travel in the management-to-employee direction: the company newspaper, the chairman's video, the employee report, the senior executives briefing, the departmental newsletter, etc ... all are concentrated on passing information down the line rather than encouraging its upward flow.

This creates problems. It's rather like getting stuck at the lunch table with Harrison from buying who's an inveterate do-ityourselfer and never fails to give a blow-by-blow account of the latest decoration scheme or patio extension at Number 23. Very soon you just stop listening and simply respond with an occasional 'Really', 'I see' and 'Very nice'. There's a lot of talk but genuine communication is absent because, ideally, true communication involves talking in *both* directions.

That communicative interchange in business and industry is hard to achieve but we must aim to make it as two-way as possible. Otherwise, those giving the information will have no idea which parts of their message (if any) are being received, and whether or not they are using the right methods. Without this feedback, we tend to lose sight of the dividing line between information and propaganda. Then our communication has no more credibility than a political broadcast – and we all know the value of those!

Stop, look and listen

We all like to *talk*. But sometimes we also have to *listen*. Sperry ran an immensely well-publicised corporate campaign in the US and later in Europe, based on that very word 'listening'. 'We understand how important it is to listen' was the tagline which went around the world. Sperry became the 'listening company'; they taught their managers how to listen first and speak afterwards – and it worked.

If we are not prepared to listen we may miss the sounds of those first faint rumblings which, unattended, will later swell into a landslide of resignations or an earthquake of stoppages and strikes. So, make the traffic two-way. The bonus of this communication flipside is that passing information *up* the line does not require the cost and elaborate media of *down* the line programmes. The essentials we need are just a spot of talking and listening.

Five main types of information come back up the line.

Complaints

At the heart of many an industrial punch-up is the fact that some or all of the employees are disgruntled about something while those at the top are blissfully unaware that anything is wrong. The complaint may be trivial, like dry fish fingers in the canteen, or something really serious like a dangerous piece of equipment or unhygienic washrooms. All too often such complaints hit a barrier on the way up – be it a bloody-minded supervisor, a hard-nosed personnel officer or an office or factory manager who's scared of head office.

Demands

Today, demands usually *are* heard at the top! But demands (and requests) for more pay, better lighting, smarter overalls or shorter hours are nevertheless all part of the two-way communication process.

Personal Information

Then there's the strictly factual information about employees and the immediate circumstances of their lives which affect their work and prospects. We're talking here about the key facts to be logged by the personnel and training departments which may run from family, financial and medical information to knowledge of special skills, qualifications and outside interests. A fine line needs to be drawn between what is common knowledge and what must remain confidential, but the more we know about those who work with us and for us, the better we should be at maintaining a good working relationship.

Opinions

There's what people think. Then there's what other people *think* they think. If the genuine attitudes, beliefs and opinions of employees are made known at the top, everyone will be that much wiser and more sympathetic.

Questions

This is where the communication system should really score. One of the most powerful benefits of organised and effective channels of internal communication is that people can get answers to their questions. If Harry in maintenance doesn't know why the super-market where his daughter works doesn't sell the company's products, then all the information about the new factory in Scunthorpe is going to flow over his head until somebody clears up that simple point. And there's no point in blitzing the Eastbourne branch with the latest video on cash flow and deferred taxes if nine-tenths of them are still trying to understand the last presenta-tion on current accounting and no one's bothered to ask them if they have any questions.

Of course, once we invite questions we have to come up with an answer – of sorts, and at times that could be embarrassing. But in most cases such questions are surprisingly simple and can be satisfactorily answered by the appropriate member of management with no loss of face or confidentiality. Once again, as with many of the communication methods we have been discussing, it is opening the channel which is important – not the quality of the material passing through.

Now, just to answer a question which may be lurking at the back of *your* mind, we're still talking about *communication* – not *consultation*. Where this book talks about dialogue it's about the two-way passing of information. It's about *what*, not about *whether*. For our purposes, the management is *telling* the employees about the new shift system and they are *asking* about the details. There are plenty of other books and experts to expound on the subjects of consultation, participation and industrial democracy.

Maintaining an upward flow

Which of the different means of communication work best for this upward flow of information from employees to management, and how are they best used?

So far the *Trade Unions* have been left out of the picture. They have several important functions, but the dissemination of management information isn't one of them. Nor should it be. No union worth its salt expects to tell its members about all the things which management want passed on. Their main task in life is to *represent* the employees and it's as *upward* communicators that the unions come into their own.

Demands and *complaints* are the two types of information you'd expect them to express to the management in no uncertain fashion. To some extent they can also ask *questions* on behalf of the employees, although the onus is then on them to go back with the answers. So questions are really best put direct from employee to manager with an equally direct response.

In general and in addition to their negotiating role, trade unions in a company can be useful for collecting and channelling material from the factory or office floor to management.

Of the other communication methods we've already discussed, some are only good at pushing information out from a small number of people to a larger number. But others do have a two-way function. For example, as we have already seen, the *company newspaper* can carry a very effective hot-line page or column in which employees can fire virtually any question at central management and receive a published reply. The local *newsletter* can also have a question-and-answer section about local matters with appropriate managers answering employees' queries.

However, in both cases we must be careful not to bypass existing procedures. The purpose is to *supplement* the employee-management chain of communication, not to undermine it. If a system exists for certain types of complaint or query to be channelled via the supervisor or shop steward it shouldn't be supplemented by a complaints column, although with general agreement such a column can improve understanding and resolve minor problems.

Although *suggestion schemes* are generally limited to ideas for improving productivity and efficiency they are still a good – and confidential – way for people to demonstrate their views on aspects of running the business. As well as the commercial benefit to the company they are an excellent encouragement to employee participation. One major company has even pioneered an extension to the suggestion scheme in which employees can raise any matter via a confidential internal form and get a personal reply from the manager concerned.

The procedural chain itself has a part to play in two-way communication, although for the most part it tends to be restricted to those written or verbal demands and complaints submitted to the supervisor or shop steward and passed upwards on what may be a tortuous and lengthy journey, only to be repeated on the way down.

Some of the methods we've been looking at in previous chapters are much more immediate. And they can cover a wider range of information.

Walking the floor

You can't beat getting off your seat and finding out for yourself. The simplest, cheapest and most effective way for managers to establish what their employees want, what they think, what they like and dislike and what makes them tick is to go and talk to them!

You need to do it with your eyes open, of course. If you go round any group of employees asking things like 'How's it going?', or 'Any problems?', there's bound to be a fair bit of old-soldiering. There'll be horror stories about how the power tools never work properly, or how the flexi-time system is unfair or the new monitor screens are giving everyone eyestrain. But the fact remains that no communication method is more effective than simply talking to people.

Meetings

Any kind of meeting is two-way by nature – or should be. The rule here is the smaller the better. At a mass meeting of the manager and 500 employees the upward communication is limited to half a dozen of the most vociferous ones hogging the scene, and at a joint works committee perhaps only a limited number of employee queries will be raised.

The ideal meetings for two-way talking are small departmental meeting or briefing groups. But even then it can be a long road from when the new shorthand typist asks her supervisor at a briefing meeting about the poor distribution of the company newspaper to when the appropriate manager brings it up with the responsible director at a similar get-together.

Formal presentations

At first sight, formal presentations are mainly a downward form of communication, of distributing information about the company to the employees. Probably the most valuable part of these presentations is the question-and-answer sessions which follow each one. This is a very specific and relevant method when it comes to people being able to put their own questions and get answers. Take the annual figures, for example. It's fine to explain them in the form of an employee report, a slide/sound presentation, a video or in the company newspaper. But none of these methods can be questioned. So it's vital that after each presentation you schedule time for questions. Some questions may be specific to finance or safety or R&D, so it's advisable to have the local management team there to answer the questions – although there are chief executives who pride themselves on being able to deal with every query themselves, from the ROA figure to the state of the gent's toilet.

When such a programme of presentations is launched, companies often find that there are few questions forthcoming and sometimes none at all. This gives an excuse to the cynics to rubbish the entire idea. However, once the presentation style is more familiar and employees are more at ease with the idea, the atmosphere is likely to change. Take heart from a factory that spent a fortune installing an employee conference room. The employees would come in, a few hundred at a time, and sit in small groups round television sets watching video presentations by the management on the figures, performance, quality, competition, and so on. The first time the management tried it, eagerly expecting a useful cross-flow of ideas and information, they got just the one question: 'Why are we using Japanese TV sets?'.

Fighting back the despair, they soldiered on. Three years later each presentation in that room attracted a good hour of searching questions. As a result production in that factory improved enormously. No one in that management would claim that the better output was all because of a few video programmes and question-and-answer sessions, but, equally, they believe it helped considerably.

As with walking the job, don't expect all the questions to be relevant to the presentation. In fact, a lot of them won't actually be questions at all, but more like statements. Such a forum inevitably provides a few trouble makers with a heaven-sent platform for having a moan and trying to make idiots of the management in front of the other employees. But the experience of those companies who have tried the two-way system suggests that, after a while, those others start to tire of the negative approach and start to ask more positive and relevant questions themselves.

'Ownership of the idea'

An invaluable technique for communicating and motivating is to encourage your 'audience' to think for themselves. For example, if you simply tell the workforce that they must improve productivity by 25 per cent you are unlikely to have much success. But you'll improve your chances if you explain that the Japanese competition will drive the firm out of business unless productivity is improved by 25 per cent. And you're most likely to succeed if they *deduce for themselves* (or at least *feel* that they've deduced for themselves) that they'll be wiped out by the Japanese if they don't do something drastic about productivity.

Here's an example of how two-way communication and 'ownership of the idea' can be made to work. Many organisations go through the annual ritual of convening the top management at a weekend conference centre and bombarding them with hours of presentations and complicated slides. Their minds befogged with an excess of preaching and informational overkill, the managers then take to the bar and the golf course as a welcome escape from the proceedings, and leave on the Sunday afternoon more confused and demoralised than when they arrived.

Imagine the difference, then, when the same top management cynics find themselves being given a presentation by the board on the company's situation and problems, and then being asked to break into syndicates (of four to eight people from different areas and departments) and spend the rest of the morning coming up with their own proposals for running the company. The after-lunch 'graveyard slot' is taken up with syndicate leaders reporting back while a director summarises the findings on a large blackboard or whiteboard. Once each syndicate has reported and there has been a general discussion on the points raised, the director then summarises and the company has the makings of a draft plan. In most respects the plan will be virtually what the board was going to do anyway, but there are three important differences:

- the syndicates will probably have come up with one or two aspects that the board hadn't thought of;
- if there are any controversial areas the board will receive early warning from the syndicates; and

- the management are now infinitely more committed to the programme than they would otherwise have been because to a certain extent it's *their* plan.

This approach can then be adapted and used for the next tier down, with the top managers convening their middle management and going through a similar exercise (and making sure that they feed any useful suggestions back up to the board). Middle managers can do something similar with their supervisors – and so on until everyone in the company feels involved in the decision-making process.

Nor does this method of communicating have to be reserved for major presentations. It also works well for smaller, *ad hoc* communication exercises.

Chapter 10
Keeping Tabs

The value of regular surveys

A record company was hard put to meet the unexpected demand for a highly esoteric LP. Sales were so dramatic for what was meant to be a limited edition that a senior executive was sent to investigate. After much travel and probing he found that the records were being bought in West Africa where the delicate plastic discs were being played at 78 rpm on old-fashioned gramophones with steel needles. It ruined the records, but produced the best tribal dance music the inhabitants had ever heard!

Nearer to home, the same could be happening to your employee communication strategy. Just because every copy of the company newspaper is snapped up on the day of issue doesn't necessarily mean that everybody is reading it. Sixteen pages of newsprint can have a totally alternative lifestyle. The very fact that such a publication is free can encourage employees to take it, but not to read it. How often have you come away from a national exhibition, staggering under a pile of brochures about cars or boats or ideal homes, which have ended up in the dustbin, unread, a week later? Perhaps some employees are grabbing a handful of copies and depriving others of theirs. Perhaps the bundle of copies never even reached that particular branch. Perhaps (and it's happened to me) the bundle *did* arrive but has been stored unopened in a dark corner of the postroom or under the receptionist's desk, never to see the light of day. So you just can't be sure.

The same is true for other media such as video or a slide presentation. So, they all sat in silence through the whole show. But did it sink in? If so, how much of it? What impression did they get of the new MD – an honest man or a villain? Were they even awake? After the show you gave out a printed summary of the information. Full marks for trying. But was it read? Did the employees appreciate the effort or see it as another piece of management propaganda? Perhaps some of them understood it while others didn't.

Communication needs monitoring to ensure that the information is getting through. Occasional surveys are essential – especially when you are trying a new method of communication. It might be counter-productive to follow up *every* issue of the company magazine with a questionnaire (although some companies do), but at least try to keep tabs to see if your efforts are working and in what ways they could be improved.

The crucial factors

There are many factors to consider. For example, regional differences play a large part in communication. It's easy to forget, sitting in a London head office, that Britain is really a mixture of different states.

The average Brummagem is as different from the average Glaswegian as a Greek is from a Frenchman. Attitudes and ways of doing things can change enormously within a few miles. And the language isn't all that common either – have you ever thought how many different words there are for 'lunch box'? This means that you can't afford to relax just because the chairman's annual message is going down a bundle in Pontypridd. For all you know they could be burning an effigy of him on Tyneside!

Then there are the 'demographics' – the different ages, jobs, length of service and ethnic groups – to consider. A good survey might reveal that the new video on the pension scheme isn't getting through to the under-25s, or that some of the long-service drivers are having a job understanding the finance director's concept of value added.

It's useful to have an idea of employee preferences in general and a survey is the best way of keeping a finger on this pulse, ensuring that the message received is the same as the one you transmitted. If you want to know something: what people like, what they want, what they need or whether they understand, why not go out and ask them? But before you go, here are some basic principles.

Use professionals

Surveying is not as simple as it sounds. For all sorts of reasons people don't necessarily say what they really mean when answering questions, so the questions need to be prepared and posed by experts. If you don't know how to set the questions, how to select a representative sample and analyse the answers, you could end up heading off down the wrong track completely and doubling the original error.

One solution may be to use the experts in your own company if you have them – the marketing or statistical department, for example. An outside firm of consultants will be more expensive, but against that you have the benefit of knowing that the survey is completely impartial.

Don't try to cover too much ground with one survey. If you want to know how your newsletter, video and suggestion schemes are going, then you're in for three surveys. To some extent you can cover one or two aspects of a related communication method while investigating another (eg employee report in conjunction with slides of the annual accounts), but as a general rule it confuses the findings – not to mention the participants – if you try to get too much out of the survey.

Don't survey the same people too often. If you need to establish two or three lots of information in a short space of time make sure the survey goes out to different groups of people.

What are you looking for?

Surveys can be expensive, and it's money down the drain if you don't know why you're conducting it in the first place. So your survey needs a purpose. Is it a particular type of communication received by everyone? Is it being understood? Is it appreciated, or preferred to other methods? Which parts need improving? Should more be done for certain groups of employees?

The bigger the better

What about size? In theory, the bigger the better. A wide survey conducted among thousands of respondents is more likely to be truly representative than one with a smaller 'survey base' where you might, for example, pick out a high percentage of female supervisors with more than ten years' service and an aversion to tabloid newspapers. But a big survey takes a great deal of time and money. The polls conducted for newspapers at election time cost tens of thousands of pounds, which you can hardly afford if you want to survey employee attitudes on different items every few months.

The experts should be able to advise on how to achieve a happy medium. Explain what you want to achieve and how much you can afford. In a company with, say, 10 000 employees in a dozen locations, you would possibly end up selecting 500 respondents in 10 places, while a 1000-strong factory would go for maybe 100 people for its sample.

Who to select?

Having decided how many people you want to survey and which locations are representative, it's essential to pick the victims out at random. One effective method is to take the total number of employees in the locations to be surveyed, and divide by the number of actual respondents you want. If you want to survey 100 people out of 1000, you end up with a factor of ten. Then you simply pick off every tenth name from personnel records.

Distribution

Having selected the participants the questionnaires should be sent to them at home. This enables them to complete it at their leisure in more relaxed surroundings, without workmates peering over their shoulders and suggesting earthy answers to questions like 'What do you do with your newsletter when you've finished with it?'

Response

Remember that if you send out 1000 questionnaires you won't get 1000 answers. Responses can vary enormously, but 30–40 per cent is about par for the course. So if you want to hear the views of 200 employees, send out 500 questionnaires.

Incentives

The response will probably be very small if you don't enclose pre-stamped or Freepost envelopes. Some companies even offer incentives such as a prize draw for the returned questionnaires. People always respond better if it's made clear to them that the survey is anonymous and confidential. However, if you then decide to run a prize draw you will have to add a non-identifiable numbered coupon to respect that confidentiality.

Types of survey

There are two main types of survey: *quantitative* and *qualitative*. Quantitative research is something like checking your car dipstick to see how much oil there is in the engine, while a qualitative survey tells you what state the oil is in.

Quantitative work is aimed at finding out how many people think how much about what. For example, by surveying 100 readers of the company newspaper you find that 32 per cent read the letters page while only 3 per cent read the editorial. That's a 'quantitative' result – and it ought to tell you something. Or you might find that a given number of people remembered a quarter of the information from the slide presentation, but remembered three-quarters of the video version. Again, it's a *quantitative* test with a clear message.

But that sort of information isn't enough on its own. The oil level on the dipstick doesn't tell you if the car was on a slope when you measured it or whether the oil needs changing. So a *qualitative* survey is carried out at the same time to give an idea of the validity of the results.

First, we will look at the quantitative approach. There are two ways of getting results.

Excuse me for a moment, but ...

We've all seen them, the researchers in the high street with a clip-board who stop every lucky soul except you. If they do pick you it always turns out they're really selling life insurance or time shares on the Costa Blanca. In much the same way, researchers can be sent round the factory or office, picking people at random, asking them the questions which have been prepared in advance and ticking the boxes accordingly. This method has two advantages.

- You get a very high response rate. It's one thing to throw a questionnaire in the waste bin, but quite another to tell someone to their face where they can put their questions.
- The same amount of attention is given to each question. People filling in a form in private often lose interest half-way through or tick boxes at random. But when the questions are put verbally most people tend to be fairly honest.

However, the disadvantages of the clip-board survey can outweigh its advantages – in industry at any rate.

- It's expensive. Ten minutes of a researcher's time costs a lot more than a couple of second class stamps.
- It's an intrusion. Many people resent being picked on and grilled by a complete stranger, especially with their colleagues around. What's more, in many companies, it can play havoc with production if employees are suddenly plucked from their workplaces.
- To cover the same numbers costs much more time and money. A questionnaire can be posted, if necessary, to a sample of thousands and the response analysed inside a few weeks. To do the same exercise with clip-boards will take a lot of people a lot of time.

The self-completion alternative

The other quantitative survey method is to distribute question-naires for the respondents to fill in themselves. These can be handed out, but usually they are posted to employees' homes to be filled at leisure. Ideally, they should include a postage-paid or Freepost envelope and the answers should be anonymous. The most common type has very simple questions with a choice of boxes to tick. For example:

> 3. *Every issue the company newspaper carries a section called 'Safety Matters'. Do you read it:*
>
> (a) *Always* ☐
> (b) *Frequently* ☐
> (c) *Occasionally* ☐
> (d) *Never* ☐

Not only is this format easier to answer, it's also much simpler for the researchers to collate afterwards. The questions can also be phrased to determine more than just the bald statistics. For instance, you might ask:

> 4. *The column 'Company Notes' is written by the editor. Do you think it is:*
>
> (a) *Biased towards management views* ☐
> (b) *Neutral* ☐
> (c) *Biased towards employee views* ☐

In fact, a questionnaire can tell you almost anything you need to know about communication – how it's received, whether it works, how it could be improved. In some areas you will want to give the respondents more scope to reflect their exact views. For example:

> | | strongly agree | agree | disagree | strongly disagree | no opinion |
> |---|---|---|---|---|---|
> | 6. *Communication is* generally good in this company. | ☐ | ☐ | ☐ | ☐ | ☐ |

As with all communication vehicles, there are pitfalls to watch out for. As Disraeli said, 'There are lies, damned lies, and statistics.' We may not be conscious of it, but there are all sorts of ways in which we can fudge the results when we fill in a questionnaire form. Examples are as follows.

- say the questionnaire is about the monthly newsletter. It's more likely to be filled in and returned by the people who read it than by those who don't. So you could end up with a set of figures which show, say, 60 per cent of *respondents* reading the New

Business column when maybe only 30 or 40 per cent of the newsletter's *recipients* actually do so.

- There's also a subconscious tendency to tick a particular box, especially if you're not sure of your answer. With an odd number of boxes the uncertain respondent will probably plump for the middle one. With even numbers and no obvious centre line, the tendency is to go for the top box.
- It's also human nature to want to please, however unintentional the thought may be. So in many cases you'll get the answers someone thought they *ought* to give, rather than what they really believed.
- And, conversely, an awkward few will always do the exact opposite and tell you what they think you *don't* want to hear, even if they're really quite happy with the situation.

In some surveys the distortions might be considerable. In others there might be little or no distortion. So the researchers test the *quality* of the results by conducting a *qualitative* survey. This is much more searching, so it's only carried out among a small sample or the cost would be prohibitive. There are two ways of tackling it.

The interview

For this approach the researcher borrows an office or visits respondents at home – by appointment preferably – and puts similar questions to those in the questionnaire. An experienced interviewer knows how to make people relax and will often discuss a particular item at length in order to dig down to the true answer (note the difference from a clip-board interview, which just asks the questions on the form and is almost entirely quantitative). After a handful of such interviews – conducted in different locations among a variety of employees – the researcher has a pretty accurate set of results to measure against the quantitative results.

Discussion groups

A more random but very informative method is to set up small discussion groups of between six and ten employees. They, too, will differ in age, sex and experience, although not in job comparability. Peer groups remove the embarrassment and reticence which tends to develop when managers and managed sit round the same table. This time the interviewer acts as facilitator and raises the various topics in the questionnaire. People soon lose their inhibitions and start to say what they really think. The discussions can be taped (with the group's agreement), or a second researcher can be present to help guide the discussion and take notes.

Keeping tabs for yourself

So far the types of survey we've discussed are best done by people with experience in this sort of work. But it doesn't stop you from getting a feel by conducting an individual, one-person survey. The principle couldn't be simpler. You go round some of the employees and find out for yourself what it is they want. There need be nothing elaborate about it – simply leave the office for a day every few weeks and talk to people. Naturally it's best to clear the way first with the local management – particularly the industrial relations team, so that they aren't put on the spot by the sudden appearance of 'one of them' wandering round the place asking questions. And it's hardly guaranteed to make you popular if you bring production or the monthly computer print-out to a crashing halt by distracting people from their jobs.

Having cleared things with the local management, the aim should be to talk to a cross-section of employees in the time available. Selection of interviewees should be both random and representative, and interviews can be conducted either at the workplace or in a borrowed office. And try to incorporate a group discussion, at which participants can unwind. Either borrow a conference room or pay a visit to the canteen.

One advantage of this sort of survey is that you can vary the questions according to any specific problems you might have. A formal survey has to ask everyone the same questions if it's to do the job properly, but the nature of your communication is probably changing all the time. Another advantage is that it's extremely cheap; costing only your time and the train fare or petrol. It's also highly flexible. If things are quiet at the office you might get through three or four sessions in a month. If you're busy you can skip it for a few months. And there's no time limit – you can keep on doing the surveys for as long as you're in the job. The greatest advantage, however, is that it gives you a gut feeling about the methods you're using. Unless you get out regularly and discuss your communication programme with the very people at whom it's aimed, then you're guilty of communicating in a vacuum. It never ceases to amaze us that responsible, highly paid in-house communicators (and some consultancies for that matter) continually commission publications, films and videos without a preliminary survey to discover the needs and perceptions of the people they're supposed to be communicating with. That's irresponsible management.

Statistically, of course, there's no substitute for a full-scale survey. On your own you can't hope to gather the sort of quantitative data that would be obtained from a few thousand questionnaires and a team of researchers. Your sample will inevitably be very small and might therefore be unrepresentative. You also have no way of knowing if the answers you get are the whole truth or simply what the interviewees want you to believe. But the statistical disadvantage is outweighed by the benefits of getting to know your audience at first hand. One effective way of getting honest answers is to discuss things in groups rather than with individuals. If, for example, you get a mixed group together in a conference room or you take the latest issue of the company newspaper into the canteen at lunchtime and sit down at a table with half a dozen employees they'll soon start to speak from the heart.

One important point for getting at what people really think is not to give them time to prepare for the interview in advance. If people are told an hour in advance that they're going to be interviewed about company communication, then no doubt they'll get hold of a copy of the annual report and do some boning up. You'll be amazed at how much they know about the company! To get a gut feeling you need gut reactions, not prepared answers.

Use the Information

The fate of many surveys is a sad one. After hundreds of hours of work, thousands of questions and scores of interviews, the results are presented to the board and published. 'That's interesting', says the Chairman, who passes it to the MD, who also finds it interesting. He passes it to the personnel director who finds it *very* interesting and passes it to his secretary to be filed.

Meanwhile the expectations of employees have been raised by the fact that management is conducting a survey. Maybe things will change at last. They don't. Two years later an enthusiastic researcher comes round on another survey and wonders why the response is so cynical. Always seek to take at least *some* action as a result of an employee survey. Tell them what the findings were – and what you've done about them, or what you are going to do. And if not, why not.

A survey achieves one of two things.

- It confirms what you suspected all along. If it's good news then by all means file it and give yourself a pat on the back, but if it uncovers any negative aspects then you should be doing something about it.
- Or it comes up with some surprises, in which case you should *definitely* be doing something about it.

The message is simple enough. If the doctor takes your pulse and it's normal, fine. But if it's pounding like a steam hammer, or has come to a halt, you don't expect him to let go of your hand and say 'Well, we'll leave it at that and take your pulse again next year, shall we?' Similarly, a survey should be undertaken with the intention of *doing something about it when the results come out.*

It should also be borne in mind that surveys in industry have many uses beyond keeping tabs on your communication programme. They are invaluable for testing attitudes on working conditions and methods, proposed changes in production or administration, management and leadership, and many other aspects of running the company.

What will it all cost?

You get what you pay for. A good consultancy could survey 300 people on a limited scale over about two weeks for £5000. At the other end of the scale, to survey 40 000 people on a wide-ranging subject once a year will cost tens of thousands of pounds.

Where to get help

Surveys are best left to the professionals if the questions are to be set and interpreted properly. If you insist on doing it yourself it'll mean a lot of training, staff and man hours (except for the one-person show). In the end it's probably as cheap to call in the experts. The first place to look is within your own company. If you have a marketing department it's more than likely that they have to conduct market research from time to time. So they may be able to recommend a company they use for market surveys, or they may even have their own research experts in-house.

Then there are the sources of general advice – the CBI, BIM, Industrial Society and your PR consultants – who may be able to recommend someone. But beware the PR consultancy that says, 'Don't worry, we'll do it for you'. Check their credentials. A very few PR firms have genuine expertise in this field. Many others don't – but claim they do. Another source can be found in the surveys you read about in the papers. Pressure groups, and others with an axe to grind, frequently commission surveys to give an independent seal of approval to their causes. We see them in the news every day : 'Three out of four directors on poverty line', 'Ninety per cent of housewives hate washing-up', and so on. The company who conducted the survey is usually named, so if you like the look of their work why not get in touch. Or you can ask for advice – and a 420 member handbook – from:

The Market Research Society
The Old Trading House
15 Northburgh Street
London EC1V 0AH
Tel 071 490 4911

Communication audits

The increasing popularity and grandiose title of the communication audit is a sad reflection on the past (and often present) inadequacies of British management. It is such a glaringly obvious discipline that every organisation should have been doing it as a matter of course for decades. Yet it is a fairly recent 'flavour of the month' approach to conducting a thorough assessment of:

- who you *should* communicate with;
- who you actually *do* communicate with;
- what you *should* be communicating;
- what you actually *are* communicating;
- how you *should* communicate with them; and
- how you actually *do* communicate with them.

The employee communication audit can be conducted in isolation or as part of an overall audit of communication with all audiences, including press, public, customers and government.

This is the sort of study that should certainly be conducted at a time of major change – new management, takeover, new policies, etc. And if you've never conducted one, why not now? It's incredible that the majority of companies continue to sail along without checking if their communication system is up to the task – or even what their communication system is in the first place!

You can seek advice on how to set about it from the employee relations section of the CBI or approach a corporate communication or employee communication specialist with experience in this field. But, as with surveys, insist on checking their credentials. A useful, if rather technical, handbook on the subject is *A Communication Audit Handbook* by Seymour Hamilton (Pitman).

Chapter 11
Case Studies

The following case studies have been selected as some of the best examples of good practical employee communication. Some are award winners, some radical, some simple. What they all have in common is that they are properly planned and executed, with adequate resources and full commitment from the top.

Whitbread

The messages from this showpiece communications programme (which won an Institute of Public Relations Award) are as follows.

- Effective communications are only a part of *good management* – but a vital part. Improved employee understanding of the company and its environment helped Whitbread achieve radical changes with minimum disruption.
- Extensive *survey* work was an important element in the programme.
- Unlike many companies who indulge in a one-off communications blitz and then wonder why it isn't working, Whitbread saw this exercise as just the beginning ...

Information

Changing social attitudes and consumer tastes calls for a quick response from both the manufacturing and service industries. The ability of an organisation to cope successfully with change is governed to a large extent by the willingness of the workforce to adapt to new ways. The brewing industry has had to undergo a radical restructuring during the past five years and to redeploy its assets to meet shifts in consumer behaviour in both the short and long term.

In 1979 it was clear to the management of Whitbread that the coming years would place great demands on both management and employees – demands that could not be met without everyone understanding the reasons that lay behind the plan to reshape the company. A poll among all employees of Whitbread in 1979 revealed how little the average person understood the basic facts upon which a company stands or falls. Nor was there much appreciation of the strength of the competition or the sort of demands from the market place that we must meet successfully. It was important to introduce a programme of 'business education' and to train all unit managers so that they would be able to brief their own people effectively.

Planning

The MORI survey was a useful starting point and highlighted the areas of weakness: for instance, how much profit the company made and what happened to it; why it was necessary to invest so heavily in the company; and where the money came from to support the capital expenditure. Clearly it was going to be necessary to develop an imaginative programme which would reach everyone at work and where possible involve the families at home. Whitbread believed that if the employees could see what the company was up against from its competitors, and could understand why business costs must be minimised and profits greatly improved, there would be a basis for better understanding in the future. A more motivated workforce was likely to be more committed.

The company newspaper, published monthly, was read by most of the employees and was the obvious channel for developing the core programme. But more had to be done if progress was to be made quickly. Television was a persuasive and entertaining medium and plans were made to use a video programme to examine the drinks market in the UK. The aim was to show how things were changing and what the company was doing to meet the new challenges.

There is nothing quite like a financial stake in the company to sharpen interest. Another part of the communications programme was to create a large body of employee shareholders. All full-time workers with three years' service qualified for the scheme.

The annual report, traditionally a full document of interest primarily to the financial community, was radically changed to present information in a more digestible form. This new style report was sent to all employees at their homes whether or not they were shareholders. Budgets were carefully assembled. The newspaper budget was unchanged and the annual report costs increased a little; savings made by keener print and paper buying helped to keep the price down.

The newspaper, the annual report and the annual video programme cost about £12 per employee each year – not a very high price to pay for a well informed workforce.

Execution

A policy committee of the Chairman, group managing director, personnel and public relations directors, meets with the editor of *Whitbread News* every month to examine the issues the newspaper should tackle. Every issue is designed to cover some important business topic written in a way that informs readers of the key economic facts. The paper is printed and despatched within three days of going to press.

The video programme is shot over a two-week period after the end of the company's financial year and issued to all locations within the company during the week following publication of the financial results, an event also covered extensively by the newspaper. A small electronic news gathering (ENG) unit is employed and the programme is shot in video. The small crew and the adaptable nature of the camera means that many locations can be covered within a sensible budget.

The annual report is produced by the public relations department and has been changed from its original form to include non-statutory pages with simplified accounts and a pinture section illustrating some of the highlights in the year under review.

Summary

The three arms of the programme are designed to work together and the effect on employees is measured by the MORI organisation every two years. The communications effort is continuous and is always stimulated by the findings of this regular poll. It is acknowledged that this will be a long haul, but there is evidence that the workforce now understands more about the demands that change imposes on a company. There is no doubt that the economic climate over the past three years had made people more receptive, but changing work practices, allied to more information about the business, have been very helpful. Changes in Whitbread have meant the closure of six breweries in three years and of several depots in different parts of the country. It has also meant a big redeployment of the workforce and some 3000 redundancies, all of which was achieved without disruption.

(This information was provided courtesy of the Institute of Public Relations).

Commercial Union

Commercial Union (CU) provides an example of how the success of a communication programme can be determined by the establishment of an effective *structure*. Here are some aspects worth noting.

- *'Ownership of information'* is an important aspect of successful communication. Instead of just being told to pass the information on, managers are made to feel involved.
- *Obtaining feedback* from the recipients of the information can be a vital part of the process.
- This is a case where the appointment of public relations consultants made an important contribution to the success of the venture. But note the *short lead time* (five weeks!) that the consultants were given for such a major project. All too often, consultants are asked to help at the last minute when they should have been called in months earlier.

Over a period of two years CU was to undergo a series of organisational changes designed to capitalise on its current success and meet the changing needs of the marketplace. In essence its network of branches was reorganising from one composite business into two specialist ones (Life and Financial Services, and General Insurance), involving the creation of 20 new offices, the closure of some and a change in reporting lines for almost all the 7000 staff. Edelman Public Relations was appointed in late September to devise and run an internal communications programme for the announcement of its new structure to all employees on 4 November.

Objectives

- To communicate the changes internally as part of a positive information process.
- To retain existing staff and in particular minimise disaffection among branch managers and the salesforce.
- To ensure that external audiences see the reorganisation as a minor evolutionary change for the better.
- To maintain total confidentiality throughout the planning phase in order to minimise rumour and inaccurate information.

Strategy

Edelman advised that the 'D-Day' approach would only be successful if branch managers themselves felt a degree of ownership for both the information and its method of communication. A two-tiered briefing process was therefore recommended: a central information seminar for the 60 senior managers; and local staff briefings by branch managers simultaneously across the country.

Edelman also recommended the creation of an overall theme for the programme. This would help to establish a sense of planned development and coherence throughout all communication over the next two years. This theme should also reflect the evolution of an already successful company to meet the needs of its future marketplace. Edelman developed the theme of 'forward from strength' which was adopted for the programme and a logo designed.

Briefing timetable

26–27 Oct	Central information seminar for branch managers (BMs).
3 Nov	Briefing of line managers by branch managers as a courtesy to their position.
4 Nov	Local staff briefings.
7 Nov	Controlled briefing of intermediaries/appointed representatives by sales personnel.

Action

Research

Edelman worked closely with CU to identify the benefits of the reorganisation for each area of operation within the company: sales, underwriting, underwriting services, claims, administration. As part of this process CU was helped in the definition of the shape of the new UK divisional structure, and the structure of the two new areas of specialisation within it.

Central co-ordination

The need for confidentiality necessitated a very short timescale between the central briefing of branch managers and the actual staff briefings. An 'action manual' was therefore devised to assist them through the process of inviting staff to the briefings, arranging rooms and refreshments. The manual contained sample material, the agreed script for their presentations, briefing analysis, and so on. In addition, Edelman provided a central co-ordination team as a focal point for any logistical queries and also to arrange the secure distribution of large quantities of confidential material to each location.

Seminar

The central information seminar combined the briefing process with the need to engender a sense of ownership of the communication programme among branch managers and also to inject a celebratory element.

Day 1:   **Presentation** (chaired by the general manager)
          The reorganisation
          Forward from strength
          The action manual

          Celebration dinner
          Opportunity for informal discussion and recognition of
          branch managers' importance.

Day 2:   **Workshop**
          Session 1: Group examination of speech guidelines for
          branch managers.
          Session 2: Group examination of questions and answers.

After the seminar the speech guidelines and question and answers
were amended to incorporate the managers' input and redistributed
within 48 hours. Edelman were given total responsibility for the
organisation of the central information seminar from making all the
travel arrangements, through to writing the presentation and workshop papers.

Local briefings

The organisation of the local briefing sessions was the responsibility
of individual managers. The action manual included suggested
formats, draft letters of invitation, sample literature, dimensions of
the display stands, slides to accompany the speech guidelines, and
an action checklist taking each manager from the day after the
seminar through to the day of their local briefing sessions. The
controlled briefing of commercial contacts was achieved solely by
those sales people in direct contact with them. A brochure was
produced to assist with this process, and a draft letter included in
the action manual.

Support material

A range of material was developed to assist managers with their
individual briefing sessions including a staff leaflet, brochure,
display stands, slide presentations, speech guidelines and a
question-and-answer brief. All material was conceived, researched,
designed, produced and distributed to managers within the
compressed five-week timeframe.

Edelman recommended the production of a special feature for
insertion in CU's quarterly newsletter *Focus*. As the first of its kind,
the insert attracted attention, and its format of 'your questions
answered' was introduced by an interview with their deputy
general manager.

Analysis

A feedback process was built into the communication programme in order to monitor employees' responses to the planned reorganisation. A briefing analysis report was included in the action manual and all managers were asked to complete these for central analysis. To assist the process, this form was put into CU's computer system for easy access and mailing. Overall, the feedback was favourable and the information and material were well received. Edelman worked closely with CU to provide answers to any new questions, and these were circulated back out to branches within three days for them to report to their staff.

Locations announcement

This feedback process identified the need for an interim stage of information about the future shape of the new network and the individual locations within it. Although it was important to fulfil the commitment to providing information as it became available, it was still too early to be precise about the timing of changes in each location and the specific effect on individuals.

The announcements were set for 16 December and Edelman devised three briefing alternatives, from which branch managers selected the approach which best suited their local requirements.

- Branch manager meetings for staff briefings at locations where changes were significant.
- Line manager meetings, to support the branch managers where several locations required personal staff briefings simultaneously.
- By letter for locations where there was minimal change.

Edelman produced briefing guidelines for insertion into the action manual and an additional checklist. An additional printed leaflet was also produced for distribution to all staff and intermediaries, indicating the location of all branches for both the Life and General sides of the company.

The budget was £120 000, including fees and production costs. It reflects the exceedingly short timeframe within which the programme was devised and carried out.

The future

The programme continues with Edelman counselling CU on how to advise individual employee categories about their changes in function, in particular ensuring a balance of skills across both specialist areas. Work will include developing a programme for launching the new offices locally to both customers and the media.

(This information was provided courtesy of the Institute of Public Relations.)

Cadbury Schweppes

Here is an example of persistence paying off. Many companies would have copped out with the familiar cry of 'It isn't working' long before the point at which Cadbury Schweppes started to get it right. But persistence and (eventually) professionalism paid handsome dividends in the long run.

Time and again employee communication textbooks stress, quite rightly, that the best way of communicating with an individual is through his immediate supervisor, and participation schemes, team briefing programmes and cascade systems ultimately rely on the company knowledge and communication skills of one person.

But what if he is simply a poor communicator? What if the department or branch or division itself is ineffective at passing on the right information? A survey will reveal these inadequacies and then training and a change of strategy will put matters right in the long term. But in the short term (and preferably as a permanent feature, for such gaps have a habit of appearing elsewhere in the structure), there must be a fail-safe method of getting key information through to the individual employee from the top.

This principle had always been accepted in the Cadbury Schweppes Group of companies where, despite a sophisticated and long-established participation framework, key financial information was displayed on pre-printed notices at every UK site at the same time it was announced to the Stock Exchange. A commentary from the Chairman, unbecomingly known as the Chairman's Red Flash, supported these bare facts and went to all managers, participation reps and site noticeboards. Divisional employee newspapers would also carry more detailed and localised stories on these facts in their subsequent issues.

By the time the annual report itself was printed the key figures of profit and loss had been given a good airing through several communication channels. What was then needed was a more far-reaching look at the company as a whole; where it was going, what it was producing, and what the figures actually meant in terms of people and their jobs.

The company participation system decided to produce a report to UK employees called, simply, *People*. It covered:

- the company's attitude to employees;
- who the company's employees were;
- employee turnover;
- time worked and lost; and
- health and safety.

The Chairman provided an introduction strongly linking this particular media format with people. 'It is concerned', he said, 'with people at work and it is on them that the company depends for its future and for its reputation.'

It was a fairly bland package with a heavy helping of facts and figures about people, although no one was actually mentioned by name and there were some forgettable statements such as, 'Various people have specific responsibility for health and safety matters in the company.' However, it looked fairly bright and readable but when it was eventually published there was a mixed reception from the joint consultative committees and the divisional and factory councils. Sites reported 'a low level of interest in the publication' and many argued it was counter-productive in terms of the current concern with cost-cutting.

Despite this somewhat lukewarm approach *People* continued, adding financial information and appearing in newspaper format rather than the former magazine style on the grounds that the publication could be printed more quickly and be in the hands of employees sooner. There was now much more included on production and results. A number of people were pictured and mentioned by name (although the names were mainly those of managers and directors), there was a divisional round-up, special features on marketing, management training and medical care, and a bright, if garish, breakdown of the main figures. Employees were even told how much each copy had cost to produce.

For the next three years the mixture continued as before but top management statements predominated and lengthened and the idea of people at work dropped out altogether. By the fifth issue the difference between its original aims and the published product had widened considerably. *People* had stagnated and the site pick-up level was falling rapidly.

By this time the control of the publication was firmly in the hands of head office – it was the Chief Executive/Chairman's report to the troops. The newly-established employee communication department took the product in hand and asked, 'What exactly is it that employees want to know about the company they work for?' They suggested:

- What happened last year?
- What is going to happen this year?
- What about the things you haven't told me?

In came a design consultant and out to employees went a new publication, six pages of A4, with a new title, a shorter Chairman's message, the divisional review with pictures of people, a new kind of pie chart, a world-wide summary, a very short Chief Executive's report, some acknowledgement that the group had competitors and something about the communication/participation structure. The response was less than enthusiastic. No one recognised that this was the new version of the old *People*. It was difficult to read and there was no full-colour. Where were the employee facts and figures? The breakdown of turnover was impossible to read. The girl pictured on the packing line was only a part-timer ... But the new broom had had its effect; it had made people think, it had broken the mould, it had stopped the stagnation.

As a result separate meetings were held with the participation group and the top management to try to define once again what it was that employees really wanted to know. Specialist consultants were brought in to tell the management that such employee reports should take into account the hopes, fears, prejudices and understanding of their target audiences. The company was encouraged to remember that employees:

- are literal minded and relate information to their own specific role in the company;
- will wish to keep promises made to customers;
- will respond to honest statements about values and goals, but will switch off to moralising and message underlining.

A new-look *People* was produced and this time the results were favourable. From all sides of the house, including the annual company conference, came the opinion that the publication was right at last – in fact, it went on to win a major industrial trophy. That, however, is not really important. What *is* important is the fact that a satisfactory communication medium was achieved only after:

- talking to people;
- making mistakes – and admitting them;
- questioning the objectives;
- bringing in experts in the field.

The re-evaluation process has continued to this day, with the sole purpose being to get as close as possible to that statement which first defined the objective of the publication back in 1976: 'It is concerned with people at work and it is on them that the company depends for its future and for its reputation.'
(This information was provided courtesy of Cadbury Schweppes.)

Allied Dunbar

Allied Dunbar provides a good example of a company successfully breaking new ground, thanks to a firm foundation in the first place. Many such experiments fail in other companies because they come as a culture shock. Of particular interest is the way that good communications – in both directions – create a sense of team spirit and commitment to the task. Note, too, that here is an organisation which has worked hard to maintain monthly team briefings.

The formal appraisal of an employee's performance by his boss is a central feature of how staff perceive the organisation they work for and how they fit into it. When it comes to more specialised means of assessing performance, there has also been an increase in objective measures, such as assessment centres. Now an even more enlightened dimension has been added to management assessment, which involves jobholders being appraised by their subordinates as well as their superiors.

As long ago as 1985, financial services group Allied Dunbar introduced this three-way approach to reviewing managers, in an attempt to foster teamwork, while also providing managers with fast, direct feedback on their effectiveness.

Called the management effectiveness questionnaire (MEQ), the system is based on the not surprising premise that managers, like anyone else, seldom see themselves as others see them; and the rather more surprising fact that managers and subordinates use different criteria to judge any one individual. 'As often as not', says John Williams, Allied Dunbar's Resourcing Director, 'a manager's subordinates are not necessarily more critical, but certainly do perceive different strengths or weaknesses than the manager's manager.'

The system can be used as a diagnostic tool at the outset, and subsequently becomes a monitoring device to track performance and attitudes. Allied Dunbar suggest it should be carried out every two years, via a questionnaire which is completed by all three parties – jobholder, jobholder's manager, and the jobholder's subordinate. One reason that MEQ works so well for Allied Dunbar is that it was not produced in isolation. It was built on the organisation's set of fundamental beliefs, which it set down as 'The Allied Dunbar Approach', and which forms the cornerstone of its management values. Allied Dunbar produced its approach in the early 1980s, before corporate mission statements became as fashionable as they are now. 'In this way, we are measuring managers against our cultural beliefs, rather than on some arbitrary set of managerial attributes', says Williams; 'it is this which ensures that the MEQ continues to work for us. The real power of the MEQ is not simply the comparative picture it presents of an individual's performance against the company's norms – although that is valuable feedback in itself – but more the openness of the whole process. We encourage the whole team – managers together with subordinates – to discuss the results and *jointly* agree an action plan to build upon strengths and address areas of weakness.'

In this way, the emphasis is on the individual manager's personal development needs, rather than the corporate drive for efficiency. It is this highly personal focus which makes the system work so well, and accounts for a take-up of two-thirds of the eligible managers in the company – even though it is a purely voluntary scheme.

Allied Dunbar have found, in fact, that the three-way appraisal system is not enough in itself to encourage a free dialogue on company issues. In 1982 it established an employee communications function within its personnel area, which has been responsible for encouraging upwards communications. As Sandy Leitch, Allied Dunbar's Managing Director, points out: 'Most enlightened organisations have attempted to address how they communicate downwards through the organisation. Our culture is built upon effective communications up, down and across the organisation, and we have always sought to be an open company.'

Evidence of such open communications abounds throughout the company; for example, its continuing diligence on monthly team briefing sessions, where local and corporate issues are cascaded down through the organisation, and the views, comments and questions from employees to those issues are fed back up through the management hierarchy to create a continuing dialogue. It has conducted two attitude surveys during the 1980s among all its employees on all aspects of the company, both as a business and as an employer; the last survey in 1987 attracted an unprecedented 94 per cent voluntary response from its 2500 employees, 86 per cent of whom declared that, taking everything into account, they enjoyed a 'fair deal' from the company.

More recently it has introduced a scheme called 'your write'. This is a combination of question-and-answer scheme, suggestion scheme, and simply an opportunity to 'sound off', in confidence and in the knowledge that a personal reply is guaranteed. Confidentiality measures intended to break down possible worries about speaking out are extensive, ranging from retyping the original comments so that handwriting cannot be recognised, to sending the reply to the correspondent's home if requested.

Says Sandy Leitch, 'These formal systems simply reflect our growth from a young, small, informal company to a large organisation encompassing around 9000 people in total. The underlying culture, built upon mutual respect and freedom to speak up, remains the same – it is part of our mission to ensure that it always does.'

(This information was provided courtesy of Allied Dunbar.)

ARCO

This is an excellent demonstration of how an employee communication programme can achieve a specific task. Interesting aspects include the following.

- Use of the right *media* for the task.
- The ability in this case to *measure results* reasonably accurately. Note, too, that the programme cost US $47 500 and saved the company US $4 500 000!
- 'Skip level' meetings are where one tier of employees meet with the relevant managers two tiers above them – thereby skipping a level of management.

The opportunity

In 1988, the management of ARCO Products Company (APC), one of ARCO's major divisions, realised that employees were creating an avalanche of unnecessary paperwork. That paperwork was costing a bundle, both in wasted working hours and storage and reproduction costs.

Specifically, the company calculated that employees generated 67 million pieces of paper per year. In addition, the company spent US $750 000 per year in record storage fees, and in excess of US $500 000 per year in rent for the floor space occupied by file cabinets. Threatened by even more waste and bureaucracy in the coming years – and taking advantage of an upcoming relocation to a new headquarters building – the organisation decided it had to do something to reduce paperwork. The intent was to do so by changing a culture that prevails in many companies – a culture where very much in the forefront is the concept of 'covering one's behind'. The result was a concentrated effort called 'Operation Cleansweep'. The audience was APC'c 2000 employees located throughout the US, with heaviest concentrations in Southern California and the state of Washington.

Goals and objectives

The main goals of Operation Cleansweep were to:

- reduce paperwork by 30 per cent, with attendant reductions in storage and reproduction costs;
- motivate employees to adopt an approach to their business designed to reduce bureaucracy.

These goals mirrored the goal of APC. Senior management (especially President George Babikian) encouraged less bureaucratic, more streamlined operations. APC officials wanted more face-to-face communication, fewer memos, and fewer meetings. Operation Cleansweep was designed to support these objectives. Management enlisted the assistance of ARCO's employee communications department to design a comprehensive communication plan that would help meet, if not exceed, the prescribed goals.

In keeping with its objectives, the campaign itself shunned paper wherever possible and, instead, used audio and video methods to alert employees to the high cost of bureaucracy. Elements of the project, including posters and an information kit, were designed to be eye-catching and innovative – not stuffy or 'corporate'. A spy motif was developed, and the project was dubbed 'Operation Cleansweep'. The plan included 'ditch-it-days' – designated days for employees to clean out their filing cabinets. The campaign also included training programmes to help employees eliminate unnecessary meetings and superfluous paperwork. Results would be measured after the campaign and would look at the number of photocopies generated, reductions in the number of filing cabinets actually in use, the volume of records sent to permanent storage, the number of forms processed, and the amount of paper ordered.

Working on the campaign, in addition to members of the employee communications department, were representatives of a graphics design firm, members of the company's outside advertising firm, and three key APC employees. The project was implemented over a six-month period at a total cost of US$47 500.

Execution and implementation

The employee communications department supervised all elements of the campaign, including production of the tapes and information kit, teaser posters, and cans of 'bomb' spray. APC arranged for distribution of all materials and orchestrated the various meetings and training programmes.

Results and evaluation

Results exceeded all expectations. To date APC has:

- destroyed more than 46 500 boxes of stored files, representing a saving of more than US$300 000 per year in storage costs;
- reduced its number of filing cabinets by more than 53 per cent, a savings of US$2.8 million in rent over the life of the company's current lease;
- reduced photocopying by as much as 45 per cent in some departments;
- implemented an approach to business that will, according to management estimates, save more than US$1.2 million per year

in the processing, printing, and storage of forms, and US$200 000 in paper costs.

In addition, the culture spawned by the programme continues to thrive. Employee groups – management and secretaries, working together – continue to identify problems and offer solutions to help reduce bureaucracy. Most importantly, according to APC Employee Relations Vice-President Mike Mullen, 'We've had a change in attitude – a sense of trust. If employees don't have numbers at hand because they don't keep as much paper around, they no longer worry about being 'shown up'. It's become okay to say, "I don't have that at my fingertips. I'll have to get that for you".'

One unexpected result came when employee communications was notified that the Operation Cleansweep poster was spotted by representatives from the Library of Congress at an Art Directors of Los Angeles Association exhibit. The poster is now ID#79024, on file at the Library of Congress in Washington, DC.

(This information was provided courtesy of IABC and David Orman of ARCO.)

Illinois Bell

This is an example of a large-scale US programme with some interesting aspects.

- Note how established employees can be *resistant to change*.
- An important message for all companies to remember – your *employees* are some of your best *ambassadors*.
- An effective employee communication programme often requires *reviewing* and *scrapping* some systems that have been there for years.
- Increasingly, *electronic mail* is a useful addition to the communications armoury.
- A significant contribution to the success of the project is described by the manager in charge: 'To achieve all this, we frequently just went ahead and did it.'

Statement of objectives and results

In order for Illinois Bell to remain successful in an increasingly competitive marketplace, the corporation undertook to change its culture and management style. An important part of this effort was to promote more open communication among all company departments and throughout all employee levels. While the change is still in process, there has been a visible culture change evident in management's support of a more open dialogue among employees.

Problem/opportunity

In the autumn of 1987, under the leadership of the employee communications division, Illinois Bell undertook a communication audit and culture study. This research clearly revealed that the beliefs and behaviours of the old Bell System days were still strong in the company three years after divestiture and that employees yearned for the way it used to be. There was little contact between people more than one level apart, or between departments. Employees expected written procedures and approvals for every assignment and were not expected to question decisions. Communication was formal.

Goals and objectives

With this knowledge, we identified the role that employee communication could play. We developed five key objectives, ways in which the employee communications division could help make the changes occur. The entire division developed a strategy for employee communication that outlined the messages, audiences and actions required to achieve each objective.

Our five long-term objectives are:

- to build a deep understanding of the business and the industry;
- to build unity between individual and corporate goals;
- to develop employees as ambassadors for the company;
- to foster interaction and teamwork among all levels of employees;
- to counsel management to create the most effective work environments to achieve company goals.

Implementation

To support these objectives, in our first year we focused on changing the communication environment and management philosophy. This involved two primary strategies.

- *Foster interaction, dialogue and personal communication.* Employees at all levels, as well as all departments and locations have to be able to question, probe, challenge and know that their ideas and knowledge are valued.
- *Focus the media on the messages and signal the change to a new culture.* We have to use new technologies, modern design and innovative approaches that embody our desired culture to ensure that key messages are heard and to develop the understanding necessary for employee support of company direction.

Then we went to work to develop the new media and our roles as counsellors to management to make it happen. Here's what we did.

Foster interaction

- Co-ordinated and implemented 154 hourly management meetings throughout the State to discuss the company's new vision and values statement. These meetings disseminated information, but more importantly, they involved 80 senior managers in developing listening skills and awoke them to the need for interactive communication. We developed a discussion guide for the managers, produced a video discussion with company officers for use at the meetings, and developed a follow-on action guide.
- Worked with operating managers to open up communication between senior managers and hourly employees, resulting in a programme of skip-level meetings.
- Conducted management philosophy study for senior management, which became the basis for the president's conference on 'managing change'.
- Co-ordinated logistics and communication content of the president's conference, resulting in senior managers' consensus on the need for a new management style, adoption of skip-level meetings and ongoing dialogue as part of the new style, and continuing individual and group efforts to put it in place.
- Supported prototype efforts in new management style.
- Expanded existing 'meet with management' concept to reach more employees. New open forum is more frequent, less formal, meets evenings, lunchtimes, before work, on-site or at local halls.
- Involved broad cross-section of employees in developing new media and strategies through use of focus groups, interviews, panels.
- Named a staff champion to represent hourly/outstate employees in media and provide counsel to management.
- Developed prototype video discussion programme, *InView*, to expand/merge/replace former programmes and to open up the communication environment.
- Developed supervisory discussion guide for *InView*.
- Eliminated a 'letters to management' programme that had lost credibility and stood as a barrier between management and hourly employees.
- Developed and implemented a programme to improve customer focus, in which individual managers spent a day with a customer service employee.

Focus the media

- Developed and began putting in place a new graphic approach for all employee media that attracted attention and sent the message of a new culture.

- Developed a highly visible central information source, *UpFront*, a bi-weekly newspaper, focused on messages that were central to the culture change needed.
- Eliminated a bi-monthly magazine that employees considered too long and too late.
- Absorbed health and safety newsletters into new newspaper.
- Absorbed most department newsletters into newspaper.
- Combined fast-news bulletins for management and hourly into a single all-employee bulletin.
- Developed statement of purpose for each medium.
- Supported production of newsletter for benefits.
- Used electronic mail to send fast news/major announcements.
- Hired technology staff member.
- Increased hard news on in-house telephone news service.

To achieve all this, we frequently just went ahead and did it. In those areas requiring higher management involvement, we used the hierarchy and presented plans, research data, mock-ups, whatever was needed, through the chains of command. Before the end of the year, senior management was coming to us for our opinion and involvement. The most significant changes that occurred were actually opportunities that arose (or were seized) as the results of our own efforts. Whenever possible, we used requests for assistance as opportunities to promote interactive communication and our 'new culture' messages and media.

Results and evaluation

Our results to date lie in having accomplished a good part of what we set out to do. We have changed the communication environment and the management philosophy. The overwhelming measure of success is the visible culture change evident in management's support of a more open dialogue and management philosophy. The president focused his annual planning conference on managing change, with the final day devoted to the new open management philosophy. At the end of that day, he empowered all senior managers to begin the dialogue with employees, beginning with skip-level meetings: 'Shazam! Go forth and do it!'

He followed this with a confirming letter, now known throughout the company as the 'Shazam Memo'. We went from plan to Shazam in less than one year. The skip-level meetings are now happening, and implementing the new philosophy was a corporate goal for 1989. Fostering open dialogue was a key corporate communication goal for 1989. The employee communications division is working with senior management to continue the momentum throughout the organisation. We are now assessing the culture to monitor early changes in beliefs and behaviours. In the interim, we have a number of 'mini-measurement' results.

- More employees attended open forum meetings in the second half of 1988 than the old programme in all of 1987. Discussion resulted in one policy change and several interdepartmental teamwork initiatives.
- A readership survey of *UpFront* indicates that 99 per cent of employees read some of it, 72 per cent read at least half of it, the average spend 20 minutes on it. Sixty-three per cent say the level of interest is good, very good or excellent.
- Telephone news line use has increased 10 per cent since July.
- The number of employees accessing the electronic mail news increased from 5248 in October to more than 13 000 in December.
- Desk top publishing system is in place, staff being retrained.

(This information was provided courtesy of IABC and Sara Foley of Illinois Bell.)

Index